Language, Culture and Identity

Edited by Torben Vestergaard

Language & Cultural Contact • 27 • 1999

Aalborg University Press

Language, Culture and Identity

ISBN 87-7307-629-5
ISSN 0908-777X

Published by
Centre for Languages and Intercultural Studies
Aalborg University
Kroghstræde 3
DK-9220 Aalborg Øst

Phone   +45 9635 9195
Fax   +45 9815 7887

www.sprog.auc.dk/csis/index.dk.html

Distribution
Aalborg University Press
Badehusvej 16
DK-9000 Aalborg

Phone   +45 9813 0915
Fax   +45 9813 4915

Layout by Bente Vestergaard
Printed in Denmark 1999 at Aalborg University

Contents

Introduction

Are people's identities an effect of their membership of linguistic, national regional and ethnic groups, and does such group membership create problems for 'intercultural communication'? This is the theme of the papers in the present volume, some of them addressing general aspects of the theme, some of them exploring it from a theoretical point of view, some of them from a pedagogical point of view, and yet others reporting empirical investigations. The papers originate in the Third Annual Conference of the Nordic Network for Intercultural Communication (NIC), which the Department of Languages and Intercultural Studies at Aalborg University hosted in November 1996. The conference focused on the theme Intercultural Communication and National Identity, and three volumes of papers dealing with specific aspects of the conference's theme have already appeared, viz. *Intercultural Encounters in Tourism* (Pinkert & Therkelsen, eds. 1997), *Interactional Perspectives on LSP* (Lassen, ed. 1997) and *Which Identity for Which Europe?* (Herrberg, ed. 1998), while two volumes are on their way: *Communicating Culture* (Andersen, ed. in press) and *Identidad y Otredad en el Mundo de Habla Hispánica* (Cristoffanini, ed. in press).

Bausinger opens his discussion with two distinct but related questions: 1) is a person's identity constant and 2) is it bound to a certain place, locality, region and country? The answer to the first question is clearly negative, as we are all of us members of various groups and therefore define ourselves, 'manage our identies' according to circumstances; for this reason he prefers to talk about a person's range of 'identity potentials'. The question of the local anchoring of identity is more complex, for while, on the one hand, globalization means a widening of horizons, on the other, it also enhances the value of local identity, and with the erosion of the importance of national borders, cultural borders gain significance. It is only from an American perspective that the prospect of 'the global village' can be looked forward to with enthusiasm, as the village in question is an American village. But even within national borders intercultural challenges are aggravated by the static view on cultural identity. Thus this view is incapable of accounting for the situation of most second and third generation immigrants. But whereas globalization undoubtedly involves tendencies towards levelling out cultural differences, these tendencies are counterbalanced in at least two areas: one is modern tourism where we expressly seek the exotic, and another example comes from popular culture, where even the cultural products that are disseminated as a result of media globalization will be given local meanings by local audiences. In the modern world the global and the local thus coexist and interact, which means that no 'culture' can claim immunity from outside influence. For this reason, such a concept as that of universal human rights, though in origin arguably an occidental one, in the long run will gain global acceptance, though perhaps with local interpretations.

Barbara Johnstone first identifies three stages in the history of studies in the communication between people who are 'different in certain ways'. Stage one she refers to as studies in *cross-cultural* communication. This tradition was founded in the one-language-one-culture model, i.e. the assumption that there is isomorphism between language, culture, nation and state. This model tends to stress the difficulties interlocutors from different linguistic or cultural backgrounds have to overcome, and in empirical work, the focus is on cases of miscommunication. But if we were inescapably trapped in our 'native' communicative patterns, this model fails to explain, in the first place, how it comes about that successful 'cross-cultural' communication occurs at all, and further, how individuals manage, over time, to acquire new communicative patterns, or, for that matter, how collective patterns change.

The next stage is *inter-cultural* communication. In the realization that the prototypical monocultural nation-state was a fiction, and that intercommunication between people from diverse backgrounds is not at all exceptional, language and culture are here seen as nested in the ethnic group rather than in the nation and state. Basically, however, intergroup communication is still seen as problem-laden, and, because of the equation between discourse and identity, the remedy is not changing one's own discourse but rather hightened sensitivity towards other's discourse patterns. For this reason, the fact that people do seem to be able to adapt their discourse patterns to situation and interlocutors is hard to accomodate within this model.

Within what Johnstone proposes to call the *multi-cultural* communication perspective, cultures and languages are not seen as meeting between but within individuals, and consequently the focus is on communication *at* rather that *across* boundaries. The unitary character of concepts like 'culture' and 'language' is questioned, as individuals have access to multiple cultures and languages, and as beliefs and ways of talking are sometimes widely shared, sometimes idiosyncratic. This point is particularly aptly illustrated by the situation of Hispanics in the US (as well as that of many immigrants in Europe, cf. Hinnenkamp forthcoming): They live in circumstances in which they can identify totally with neither the culture traditionally associated with the standard form of the majority language around them (English) nor that of the standard form af their ancestral language (Castillian Spanish), and they therefore mix the languages to create a form capable of expressing their identity.

Claire Kramsch likewise sees the early phases of cross- and intercultural communication studies as marked by a tendency to see cultural and linguistic boundaries as more well-defined than they actually are. This she puts down to the structuralist heritage and its predilection for discrete categories and dichotomies. Instead she calls for a post-structuralist 'third stance', inspired by the American philosopher Peirce, the Russian literary theorist Bakhtin and the Indian British cultural critic Bhabha. In this post-structuralist paradigm, the distinction between ego and alter is not absolute in that we construct our own identities through categories set by others, and moreover, it is in referring to the outside world that the speaker constitutes himself as a subject. Communication is seen as 'the relational making of signs, the responsive construction of self, and the interdependence of opposites', and it is this intrinsically contradictory nature of meaning and identity that constitutes the position that we call inter- or cross-cultural. Kramsch backs up her theoretical discussion with observations from a discussion between a group of teachers of German from Germany, the US and France. When one of the Germans suggested that the image of a clock showing five to twelve overlaid with a giant swastica could form a suitable background for teaching German to Americans, the reaction of the Americans was shock and indignation; not because they did not understand the meaning of the sign 'beware of neonazis!', but because it could be related to conflicting interpretants, 'taboo' and 'warning' respectively. In the ensuing debate, the participants now resemiotize the original sign in different ways and try to solve the conflict by drawing on the communicative potentials both of the various languages available to them and of the different discourses that, in the past, have played a role in the socialization of each of them. In this way they demonstrate how there always is 'an-Other perspective to dualistic confrontations'. This is overlooked in a notion like intercultural competence, and Kramsch therefore prefers to talk of an 'intercultural stance'.

In spite of the arguments for a third stance between ego and alter propounded by Bausinger, Johnstone and Kramsch, it is a common everyday experience that different meanings – or perhaps rather, different values – will be ascribed to the same words and actions by different people (cf. the swastica example above), and that the gut feeling often is that this can be put down to differences in culture. Although Øyvind Dahl agrees that cultural codes are not fixed objects but are enacted in communication, his experiences in Madagascar have nevertheless made him feel a need for a 'Meaning Matrix', a tool for analysing the communication process when representatives of two different cultures meet. Drawing on both semiotic and sociological schools of communication, the meaning matrix first identifies the denotative content of the communication, then inserts it in the relevant contextual frame of reference, and finally interprets its connotations against the background of the context.

With internationalzation the ability to interact with people from foreign cultures becomes an increasingly important learning objective in many degree courses, and accordingly there is also a need to assess intercultural competence. But, Kirsten Jæger observes, there is by no means agreement about how this should be done, and the question arises whether the problems in assessing intercultural competence indicate more basic problems with intercultural competence as a learning objective as such. Jæger suggests a double answer: in the first place the target should not be the native speaker but 'the intercultural speaker', and second, what is effectively assessed in traditional exam situations is not competence but performance. Intercultural competence also involves the ability to reflect on one's own behaviour, and is best assessed in connection with work placements abroad.

In the second pedagogical paper, Karen Risager explores the culture–language link in language teaching. Culture is relevant in relation to language in three ways: first culture is directly reflected *in* language, in pronominal systems, politeness features, discourse conventions, vocabulary, etc. Second, culture is a context *for* language teaching in that any language has developed in and with a certain cultural context – the national culture. As a reflex of this, language teaching has traditionally attempted to re-create that context as a context for teaching, but as language use today is increasingly disconnected from that context, Risager argues that other contexts and other varieties than the standard should gain access to language classes. Finally, culture is also the subject matter *of* language teaching, and continuing the preceding argument, Risager recommends that teaching materials should to an increasing extent comprise other 'texts' than the national literature.

Inge Degn's study of the identity question in French speaking Belgium offers excellent support for Kramsch's warning against seeing the world in dichotomies. In the first place, Belgium comprises not just two but three linguistically defined communities: Dutch, French and German, which we often tend to forget, but what is more, the French speaking community is not a homogeneous unity set off from the rest. In terms of region, francophone Belgians constitute at least two groups, Walloons and Brusselers, but people also identify themselves in response to demands and pressures from outside, and in terms of attitude to the Belgian state, as many as four groups stand out: 'the French' who see themselves as part of the greater French *ethnie*, 'the Belgians', whose point of identification is the traditional nation-state in spite of the drift towards federalization; 'the Walloons', who give priority to the regional level over the national; and finally 'the post-nationalists', who point to the Belgian experience of political unity and cultural diversity as a model for Europe.

Changing the focus from Belgium at large to the microcosm of a postgraduate college for students from all over Europe, Jim O'Driscoll asks what language choice says about speakers and their attitudes to each other in situations where more than one language are available. Students were asked to report their own language use in dyadic interactions with their fellow students, and it appeared, not surprisingly, that only English and French were used as link languages. More surprisingly, students often claim to use their interlocutors' L1, but this is not corroborated: students avoid using their own L1 even when addressed in it. This in turn puts native speakers of English at an interactional disadvantage, since English is the default choice. Finally, although (or because?) English is the general language of wider communication, French became the prestige lingua franca in the college. O'Driscoll's study thus questions received ideas of High and Low languages (cf. Fishman 1971), the cultural value of speaking one's L1 in L1 – L2 interactions, and documents, among the future European elite, at least, a countertendency away form the increasing use of English.

In her exploration of the role of culture in business take-overs, Søderberg, too, notes the necessity of a multifaceted view of culture as each of us is a member of several cultural groups, possibly with mutually incompatible values and attitudes. Moreover, predictions made by too static theories of culture often turn out not to hold. Thus in cases of foreign company acquisitions, interviewees rarely ascribe difficulties to national cultures, and even at the level of organizational culture, deterministic theories of culture often fail to explain the actual successes and failures. Søderberg puts this down to two factors: a) at company level, too, there is not just one culture but many subcultures, for instance along professional, generational and gender lines; b) circumstances differ from case to case, so that concern for positive face, 'involvement', may be productive in one situation, whereas concern for negative face, 'independence', may be what is called for in another. Consequently Søderberg argues for a relational and process-oriented approach to cultural analysis.

In spite of their diversity in scope and outlook, the nine papers presented here agree on one fundamental issue: the language – identity – culture complex is seen not as static and isomorphic, but as dynamic and overlapping. In the first place, an objectivist view of culture was probably never theoretically sound, but with internationalization and the opening of political and cultural boundaries, its empirical validity is becoming increasingly questionable. In this way languages and cultures can become resources rather than homogenizing straitjackets. Finally many of the contributors touch upon the political implications of a relational and dynamic view on language and culture: for human rights in the world at large as well as for the role of local and regional cultural identities in a Europe with crumbling national boundaries.

References

Andersen, Karsten Gramkow, ed. (in press). *Communicating Culture*. Aalborg: Aalborg University Press.

Cristoffanini, Pablo, ed. (in press). *Identidad y Otredad en el Mundo de Habla Hispánica*. Mexico City: Unam.

Fishman, J.A. 1971. The sociology of language: An interdisciplinary social science approach to language in society. In: Fishman, J.A. ed. *Advances in the Sociology of Language*, Vol. I, pp 217-404.

Herrberg, Antje, ed. 1998. *Which Identity for Which Europe?* Aalborg: Aalborg University Press.

Hinnenkamp, V. (forthcoming). The poetics of codeswitching. The language mixing of adolescent 'immigrants' in Germany. *Journal of Sociolinguistics*.

Lassen, Inger, ed. 1997. *Interactional Perspectives on LSP*. Aalborg: Aalborg University Press.

Pinkert, Ernst Ullrich & Anette Therkelsen, eds. 1997. *Intercultural Encounters in Tourism*. Aalborg: Aalborg University Press.

Intercultural Demands and Cultural Identity

Herman Bausinger

Globalization: For a couple of years, this catchword has turned up more and more in newspaper headlines and articles but also in academic considerations. The sense of the word seems to be evident. There is a world wide web (I use this internet-term in a more general sense) of networks which enables us to get into contact with people in other parts of the world; through the media, the world has entered our living-rooms; economic decisions refer to all countries; mobility has increased and is no longer kept in check and controlled by borders and demarcations; there is intercontinental traffic not only by persons but also of meanings; and regional conflicts and wars can only by ended by international efforts.

Some people – not least Americans – speak about globalization enthusiastically and with unbroken optimism. They denounce traditional borders and restrictions; their identity, if any, is a floating and changing one. The present coherence and interrelation of the whole world have led a couple of scientists and philosophers to propagate not only the free flow but also the enforced exchange of everything. In our modern world, they say, there is such a high degree of mobility that a firm and more or less unchangeable identity is nothing but a prison, dysfunctional for the fulfilment of the real needs and demands of society. Vilêm Flusser, a famous philosopher of communication, regarded the allegiance to a certain place, the feeling of being at home within a city or region or country, as an outmoded attitude. Technological development, he stated, has been so effective that one doesn't need an areal embedding, a bond with certain places. He emphasized that he felt at home everywhere in the world – everywhere where he had good friends.

I hold that we should take even such a pointed and extreme statement very seriously. We have, however, to take into account the opposite attitude and evaluation. For many people globalization is first and foremost a post-modern slogan. Of course, they will not and cannot doubt that new technologies have brought different parts of the world closer to each other and that political and economic concepts have to take into consideration world-wide systems of power – but they will reduce the problem to these special fields. Life, they will say, everyday life, our trivial forms of communication and living, are still shaped by our national, regional, local traditions – here is the basis of our real identity. The idea which suggests itself (and which is not totally wrong) is: cultural identity as against economical and technical globalization.

Schematically these pairs of opposites might be reduced to a formula:

$$globalization\ (+) \dashrightarrow cultural\ identity\ (-)$$
$$globalization\ (-) \dashrightarrow cultural\ identity\ (+)$$

This formula is easy to understand and easy to handle. But although nobody will deny that the reduction of complexity is an important aim of scientific endeavours, we have to examine what has been cut off and conjured away by this reduction – and that is what I am going to do.

Before looking at some practical events and developments I shall try to arrive at a more elaborated view of my central terms: *globalization* and *cultural identity*.

As to globalization, one has to be aware that this is an exaggerating and over-generalising term. Many of the tendencies and processes called global do not really concern the whole globe but only parts of it. Developments called global are often limited to intermediary units – e.g. the Nordic countries, Europe, the Western world (which is not *the* world, but part of the world). Thus, we should rather speak of transnational or intercultural needs, steps and developments.

Secondly, globalization sounds like a natural and neutral process of diffusion – whereas, actually, it is always a question of influence, power and mostly wealth. When North Americans speak optimistically of the global village (pretending that the one world is, or will be like, one big village), they are seduced to do this by the fact that this global village is, or would be, an American village. There are critical terms, equivalents to globalization, which disclose this background: e.g. when people speak of coca-colonization (combining Coke and colonization) or Mc-Donaldization.

Thirdly, so-called globalization processes are not unbroken and linear. By and during the course of globalization, things and meanings are modified. This is even true for technical processes. A machine or a computer installed in Scandinavia is different from a machine or a computer installed somewhere in South Asia or Latin America – not as to its material substance but regarding its meaning and its social status and so on. To give an example: Indian engineers have been busy for a long time erecting purification plants for the river Ganges which is infected with coli germs – but it is very hard work for them, not because of any technical problems but because people will bathe in the holy water and (what makes things even more difficult) as a rule don't even get sick.

This example demonstrates that a clear separation of economic tendencies on one hand and cultural development on the other doesn't work; cultural experiences are intertwined with other, political, economic, technical ones.
So what about *culture* and *cultural identity?*
The term *identity* evokes associations of firm and unchangeable attachments. The archetype seems to be the *identity card* which shows and gives testimony of the unambiguous identity of its bearer. ID cards and passports refer to the nationality of their bearers – this seems to be a sort of nucleus of her or his identity . Now, this is the bureaucratic dimension of the term. But even in this dimension the definition is not so unambiguous. A person is born at a certain place, lives at a different place – he or she is not only a Dane but an Aalborg Dane from Copenhagen and as an Aalborg person, an inhabitant of Jutland.
The Austrian sociologist Manfred Prisching speaks about graded identity potentials. In the more static past, identity was structured in concentric circles: family, neighbourhood, village or town, region, nation. In our more complex society, we have to deal with the complex constitution of an identity by combining concurrent partial identities respectively identity offers not only of certain places but also of groups, of class, age and gender – this means: identity is far more dynamic, flexible and subject to change.
One could even say that the very notion of identity is a product of change. It is by changing conditions and constellations that the problem of identity is called into question. In my home region, people used to tell a little story about a carrier who drove his coach, his carriage to the neighbouring city every second day. His horses knew the way quite well – thus, the carrier used to nod off a bit on his coachman's seat and, having gone halfway, took a break and fell asleep for some time. One day he woke up – and there were no horses. He rubbed his eyes and said slowly and thoughtfully: *Is this me – or is this not me? If it's me, they've stolen my horses; if it's not me, I've found a coach.*
This is a very sophisticated and philosophical anecdote – an anecdote on identity, on a crisis of identity. Identity, as a rule, is just there, included in the naturalness of one's life. But it has to be readjusted, if there is a new situation with a new challenge. In complex societies like ours there is a great variety of specialized systems people have to get along with, and they have to take an attitude towards different collectives and their identification offers – this results in a complex structure and a plural strategy to save and protect identity or identities.
I repeat: *structure* and *strategy.* Every person handles or manages – consciously or subconsciously – his or her identity; identity is not only a simple function of the material conditions of life. A person may live for a long time in a far distant

country to which he owes his living – but nevertheless his identity may adhere primarily to his home country and region – this is or was for instance the case with emigrants. For them, identity was often an alternative and counterbalance to their real surroundings and everyday life.

This function of counterbalance can explain why identity – the term identity as well as the feeling the term represents – has become so pivotal in a time which seems to destroy and deny all narrow affiliations and which seems to dissolve all senses of belonging, in the endless sea of globality.

There is a certain necessity involved in the widening of identity horizons – but it is not a simple transfer from narrow to greater adherences and identities; quite often the wider orientation brings an increase in value of the more narrow connections. The nation building process in the 19th century did not do away with the sympathies for the respective regions and home towns – the idea of Heimat, homeland, had its boom at the same time, counterbalancing the natio- nal movements.

A comparable tendency can be discovered nowadays. The development is not the same with all people. Some people 'travel business class through the world and have created their own, safe and secure transit spaces'; others 'move all the time but are safely anchored' in their local and regional identity. For the majority of people, the horizons have widened, but this has not devalued their old loyalties and identities. As Orvar Löfgren, a Swedish ethnologist, has put it: 'More global, more regional, more local.'

The chance to step out into greater parts of the world (either literally by tourism or figuratively by media etc.) has given the home places a special reputation and additional attractiveness. The abolition or at least lifting of political borders has provoked the emphasising of *cultural borders*, the reinstatement of borders as borders of language, customs and folkways. The free-floating mobility of men has led to a new acceptance and even praise of home places, to a reflexive reinforcement of cultural descent and origin.

This sounds rather harmonious and complementary: We love our home and country – and from this experience we are able to embrace the world. And: We get hold of the whole world – and this stabilizes and intensifies our more nar- row identities, the love of our country, region, town.

Now, such generous feelings are not only utopian, but they are not average either. Very often, the emotional retreat to home place, descent and origin is not compatible with openness and tolerance, but leads the way to self-complacent and self-righteous collective demarcations and aggressions. This has been the background for the terrible clashes in South Eastern and East Europe. But what has happened there is only the pathological version of developments and tendencies which are a constant threat in many parts of the world, Europe included.

Ethnologists and folklorists, who lovingly fostered the adherence to region and country for a long time, have in the meantime lost their naivity in that respect. At least the more sensitive scholars hear a warning alarm signal whenever the word *ethnic* turns up: It pretends to give an innocent and clear description of facts, a depiction of natural traits – but *ethnicity* is not a natural quality, it is a political and cultural construction.

If *cultural identity* is treated as equivalent to *ethnic identity*, this seems to be a sensitive adjustment to the core feelings, thoughts and values of the people – but in reality it is a quite dangerous reduction. It spoils the necessary widening of the horizons and it interferes with intercultural demands.

Let me give a few examples which may show how complicated and sometimes paradoxical the problem of cultural identity in a globalized world is. First, I will treat in more detail the problem of international sport and its national implications.

After the world championship in football/soccer in 1994 and after the Olympic Games in the United States there was a lot of criticism not only regarding the shortcomings of organization, but the idea of the competition itself. The critics presented clear and irrefutable statistical tables. There were 24 teams in the football World Cup – 13 came from Europe, 6 from America, only 3 from Africa, 1 from Asia – and there is one left: Saudi-Arabia, somewhat between two continents. This is a very unequal distribution. Of course, there were qualifying contests – but the criticism was that only sports with Western superiority are organized as great world events.

There was a similar calculation for the Olympic Games. Of all the hundreds of medal winners from 1948 (London) till 1988 (Seoul) about 80% came from the USA, the Soviet Union, Great Britain and the two German states – that is from very few nations with about 10% of the world population. In the meantime, things have changed a bit; for instance China reached the high ranks, and it has about 15% of the world population.

Nevertheless: there *is* still a disparity. Well, say people in America and Europe, the most competent win, and the highest level of competence seems to be here. But is this statement sufficient? Assume that Danish fishermen were challenged to participate in a climbing championship in the high mountains, one would call this nonsense and not a fair competition. And critics hold that the world-wide invitation to the Olympic Games is a similar case. There are, to be sure, certain forms of physical exercises all over the world – but they are very different from *sport*: Many are non-competitive, many are more playful, and many are integrated into religious rites. These forms of physical training and exertion represent more *and* less than our sport – there are no elaborate gadgets and pieces of equipment which have become so important for modern sports.

This is a correct description of the traditional differences. But it is, to a certain degree, a description of the past. Latin American, African and Eastern cultures are on the way to becoming more modern states and societies. If they join modern events of sporting competition, this can be looked at as a betrayal of their traditional rituals – but, in practice, it is part of the modernization process. Western societies have gone through the same development: modern sport was preceded by primitive demonstrations of physical strength and very simple games and competitions. Nobody would call for the inclusion of – let's say , Bavarian finger-wrestling or folk dancing in the list of Olympic disciplines.

Okay, critics say – but with us this was an organic development, not an act of colonization and infiltration. I'm not that sure about this. On the whole continent, sport was an import from England, and there were vigorous debates and almost battles between the supporters of a more traditional physical training (in Germany and Scandinavia mainly gymnastics) and the propagandists of modern sports. In Germany, this war, led by the traditionalists with nationalist overtones, lasted about 150 years and wasn't settled until the middle of our century.

So why should we prevent other nations and cultures from going a similar way? Certainly, we have no right to impose modern sport on them – but neither have we the right to make the rest of the world a big open-air museum where people have to live according to their old beliefs and traditions only. The question whether sports are suitable for African or Asian people has to be answered by themselves. And they have started to give very impressive practical answers – very soon the statisticians will reveal a new problem: European and American dominance will be lost if the Western teams are not able to improve their capacity by exotic imports. The best-known and most successful Danish sportsman in athletics is Wilson Kipketer – who is not of Viking descent.

The case of Mr. Kipketer shows that transcultural demands are not just a matter of export and foreign affairs in which the Foreign Ministry and maybe some ethnologists are competent – it is also an import problem. There are *inter-cultural* demands within our own countries.

The situation of working migrants, who constitute considerable minorities in many of the highly industrialized European countries, provides an opportunity to have a close look at the problems of ethnicity and cultural identity. In Germany and, as far as I know, in other countries, too, the migrants were for a long time regarded as guest workers. They were supposed to go back after a short time, and most of the guest workers thought this themselves. They lived out of a suitcase for months and even years. When it became evident that many of them would not return (at least not quickly) an alternative was discussed: They could try to become Germans by adopting German ways of life including language, customs, education, religion. It was a modification of the American melting pot idea although the newcomers were not regarded as real immigrants by law.

But just as this design had failed in America where immigrant groups built solid retreats in the form of ethnic colonies, there was no real chance for a far-reaching assimilation process in Germany. On the one hand because the German authorities didn't develop any measures to make assimilation easier – on the other hand, however, because the migrant workers and their families needed the support and backing of their own culture more than at home. They needed the social network of their compatriots, needed familiar and trustworthy institutions, and they needed the cultural signs and symbols to give them a feeling of closeness and intimacy.

Consequently, in the 80s the idea of *cultural identity* gained ground – not only among the persons concerned themselves but also among scientists, in the discourses of sociologists and anthropologists who were attentive to these problems. The idea was that notwithstanding the necessary adaptation to working conditions and to the more technical and institutional sides of everyday life, the migrants should be allowed and even encouraged to preserve their own culture, to stay in the firm and traditional cultural identities they had brought with them. This seems to be a liberal solution, and, no doubt, in comparison with a strict assimilation program, it represented progress.

But nevertheless, this program very soon proved to be questionable, too. It became clear that the contents and fabric of cultural identity were prescribed by powerful minorities within the minorities. With considerable rigidity they urged people to return to customs and beliefs which had been done away with previously. In several cases, fissures across a culture have been bridged very arbitrarily by imposing the culture of one part of a country on the inhabitants of other parts – e.g. Turkish identity was applied to all people coming from Turkey including the Kurds, who have a culture of their own and are making exertions to arrive at a status of political independence. And the Kurds – to make things even more complicated – as a rule referred to as an ethnic unit, have different branches, too, for instance in respect of their religion and even their language; in Eastern Turkey, there is a minority group called Zazaki with its own language, Zaza.

But even where ethnic differences were less evident and less problematic, remarkable difficulties turned up along with the construction and confirmation of cultural identity. This identity framework was accepted by older people for whom it was a sort of comforting continuation of what they had experienced at home. But it was also imposed on the members of the younger generations, and at least some of them began to feel as if they were in a cultural cage. Many of them have grown up in Germany, which for them is foreign and familiar at the same time. They don't want to be just Germans, but they are no longer Turks or Sicilians or Greeks, at least not by the measures their parents and grandparents apply to these terms. They are in an *in-between* position and mood. For some, the consequences of this intermediate situation are regrettable shortcomings, starting with their linguistic abilities and capacities – some are not at all bilingual but half-lingual in both tongues.

But on the other hand, some (and not only a few) have been able to establish a new identity which is put together of elements from both sides and also mixtures, sometimes resulting in very impressive patchwork. Some years ago, in my hometown, there was a poetry competition for young foreign authors. One of the winners, a young Turkish woman, started her poem with the line: '*I am a bastard...*' Now, in German *bastard* has a negative connotation. But she called herself proudly a bastard, showing her competence to integrate elements and stimuli from both sides, arriving at an individual construction of identity which, however, is shared by other fellows and girls and, thus, is on the way to a collective identity .

The situation of those younger people coming from far away but more or less resolved to stay in their new and second home place gives reason to call to mind Salman Rushdie's positive qualification of hybrid tendencies in people and their culture. In defence of his novel 'Satanic Verses' Salman Rushdie has argued for the acknowledgement of the fusion and mixtures of peoples and cultures:

"The Satanic Verses celebrate hybridity, impurity, intermingling, the transformation that comes of new and unexpected combinations of human beings, cultures, ideas, politics, songs. It rejoices in mongrelization and fears the absolutism of the Pure. Melange, hotchpotch, a bit of this and a bit of that is how newness enters the world. It is the great possibility that mass migration gives the world."

This is a very pointed assessment and conclusion. Probably, a few years ago the expression *absolutism of the Pure* would have sounded just strange and incomprehensible. But thinking of the cleansing acts in parts of Eastern and especially South Eastern Europe, where making pure means the expulsion, deportation or death of the 'impure' parts of the population, Rushdie's position looks far more reasonable and opens a new perspective to the so-called ethnicity and to the problem of cultural identity.

In the continuing debate on the future of migrant workers and their children, politicians and culturologists for the most part are still on the look-out for general solutions: there is almost a trench warfare of identity and inbetween contestants. But this cannot but end in a draw. For the real solution is a sensible balancing out of the two positions, or in other words: it is the tolerant acceptance of different identity constructs, the acknowledgement of the *cultural autonomy* of everybody.

I have stressed the usefulness of, and the need for, *intercultural exchange,* even for mixtures and hybridity. I admit that this is a dialectical position – more often than not, if the cue *identity* turns up, people speak and think of a very firm and immovable substance and not of a plastic and workable quality, a changeable construction. I know, however, that the point of view that people don't need a firm position and fixed lines of orientation and that they are able to adapt to changing situations without loss and have at their disposal new partners and friends everywhere in the world without any restrictions is, to a certain degree, a jet-set invention, an elitist attitude. Even now and even in mobile Europe, the majority of people live in a place, in a village or town, in a region and in a country, and I think it is a fair and acceptable condition that they wish to feel at home there, and to have in common with their neighbours and fellow-countrymen norms, values and cultural objectivations and traditions. The reduction of differences, which is, to a certain degree, unavoidable in the 'one world' we have lived in for a couple of years or decades, is not the full and only answer to the challenges of modernity.

Modern life is characterized by a lack of transparency, by irritating cross-pressures and by complex structures. The ways of life are no longer marked and paved but have to be worked out and opened anew again and again. That means the liberty to decide but, at the same time, insecurity. And this fosters the need of transparent configurations, stable social relations and networks, but also a stable and trustworthy cultural background. It is primarily this need which provokes and produces the longing for, and the consciousness of, a firm *cultural identity*. The problem and task is to co-ordinate and reconcile transcultural demands and cultural identity.

There are fields in which tendencies to do away with cultural differences cannot be accepted. I will mention two.

First, modern tourism. It arose by the discovery of cultural differences; the early travellers and tourists intended to get into contact with strange people and become acquainted with foreign landscapes, customs, life styles. But tourism became an international institution and industry and, as such, tends to level out cultural differences. Today, many travellers move on *the beaten track* (to quote the title of an American book on modern tourism); they pay for standardized trips, live for some days or weeks in the monotonous luxury of international hotels.

For a couple of years many, regions have stood up against this levelling out and have stressed their specific cultural countenance – sometimes in a questionable discount mode by means of folklorization, but sometimes also by solid and sober ways of safeguarding landscapes and traditions. In this case, the effect is often quite positive for tourism – in spite of all standardization tendencies, tourists still seek strange, peculiar and specific regions.

A second example, even more influential than tourism, is provided by the *media* and their emissions. There is, no doubt, a *media globalism*. Media technology is a field where globalization is definitely happening, and this is not only a matter of free technical access and disposal and of industrial extension – it is also a matter of content: the same news and stories and series are sent to many parts of the world by mighty companies. Now, surely, there is a certain counterbalance in the filters and rearrangements of the contents by audience perception. Media scholars state that for instance American series like *Dallas* and *Dynasty* are transformed by the audiences into a German or Danish or Greek *Dallas* or *Dynasty*. This is an important reference to the active potential of passive audiences. But it appears to be a bit like an alibi argument, and what is (re)produced by the audiences is a new version – but still a version of an American film.

It is true that even media globalism has to be looked at in relative terms. Nevertheless, consumers all over the world (or almost all over the world) are swamped with the products of big production factories, and this makes it not only understandable but praiseworthy that the different countries at least try to develop their own programmes and promote cultural identity in a national framework.

Consciousness of the one world and concern for the closer forms of identity – this is not a contrast but a correlation of mutual requirements. Whenever a new and greater unit appeared on the horizon, it worked and succeeded only if it showed consideration for the existing smaller units. I haven't got a firm grasp of Danish history – thus let me turn to German history which provides very convincing examples of this.

Up to the 19th century, Germany consisted of hundreds of small, sometimes tiny territories, and it was only through the Napoleonic reforms that these small states disappeared from the map and made way for what in Germany has been called *Länder* – greater regions like Prussia, Holstein, Mecklenburg, Württemberg. The new units worked well and won people over, if the governments respected the old structures and loyalties as to religion, tradition and other specific traits. There were great difficulties, however, when kings and dukes tried to give their countries a uniform structure without consideration for the historical formation of different areas.

When the step was finally taken to found a German nation, it worked from the very beginning. One reason for this was the enmity towards France and the experience of the military victory which welded together the different parts of Germany, but another was the fact that the constitution reserved great influences and, above all, full competence in cultural affairs to the Länder.

I think it is not only a mechanical extrapolation if I apply this to *Europe.* Some passionate and rash politicians think of the new Europe as a sort of melting pot – this was the idea and strategy in the United States which didn't even work over there. But in Europe, not only people of different descent have to come, and possibly grow, together but distinct *nation states*. Thus, an optimistic model of the USE looks different: it is not a melting pot, but a sort of Easter nest. I hope you can imagine my picture: There is a basket of tightly interlaced and uniform fabric symbolising the network of institutional connections, political co-operation and economic interrelation – providing a mossy padding for what's in the basket. And in the basket, there are a number of smooth, coloured Easter eggs, each in a different colour, a gay demonstration of variety. It is hardly necessary to interpret this picture: there is a concentration of political and economic power (the basket) protecting cultural diversity (the eggs).

No doubt, the laws of politics and economy are different from the cultural contexts. In one of the publicity leaflets of the Council of Europe there is a schematic sketch depicting a person who starts a journey with 50,000 marks in his/her pocket, crosses 12 national borders and has his or her money changed into the respective national currencies. At the end of this European journey the person has reduced his or her fortune by about half, 25,000, without having bought anything – a good argument for a unified economy and a European currency. But it is different with cultural assets. They will be increased by crossing borders, increased by the interests of encounter, of learning, of a broadened horizon.

This is an argument which fits into our symbolic comparison: The coloured eggs should be preserved; unmetaphorically: national cultures (and this doesn't only refer to the achievements of art but to the ways of life in general) should be acknowledged and respected in the European Union. At the same time, one has to be aware (now I am going to produce scrambled eggs) that a national culture is more a reductive idea than a reality. In reality it is a complex fabric of different, sometimes even antagonistic, elements and all national cultures in Europe (I have tried to indicate this) include little islands of strangers, include foreign elements, but also the specific coinings of class, age and gender. If you look at a stylish young man, a yuppie in Copenhagen and at a farmer's wife in the loneliness of a little Danish hamlet, you can feel the tension in the concept of a unique national culture.

One world and *more narrow identities* – I have emphasized mutual requirements and interdependency. Thus, finally, I'd like to indicate that cultural identity for a nation is in danger of becoming a fake identity if it doesn't transcend itself and include the respect and the responsibility for what is going on beyond. There are elements of a potential globalization which are more important than the Olympic Games and the convergence of television productions all over the world.

If for instance *human rights* are put up for discussion, the retreat to national peculiarities and the specific national identity is blocked off. The concept of human rights and human dignity aims at a human identity beyond and above all cultural differences. I will not content myself with a pathetic incantation but at least mention the problems.

One of the problems is contained in the fact that the very idea of universal human rights is probably not a universal idea but an occidental one – this was the opinion held by Max Weber. But the confrontation of cultures by worldwide communication has at least produced a certain sensitivity for this idea and its topicality in many parts of the world.

There is, however, the next big problem at hand: The concrete concepts of human rights and human dignity are not uniform but dependent on the respective cultural views. An important consequence of this is that one has to get involved with these specific views and that human rights cannot be declared but in the long run have to be negotiated.

This does not mean that for instance the exclusion of women from rights or cruel punishments have to be accepted as expressions of cultural diversity. It means that cultural structures threatening human rights have to be analysed carefully.

In any case, the fashionable praise of cultural diversity and ethnic specificity is not sufficient. I think that in this context even the concept of *culture* (thought of as a firm structure) has to be called into question. No culture is an island; it is always a field of cross-pressures, a complex structure of traditional coining *and* modifying answers to new challenges. I would add, that it is not sufficient either, to make an ethological and phylogenetic retreat into the alleged deep structure and biologically determined instincts of men which – as several biologists and philosophers hold – make them unfit for continual peace and dignity. Man is a being able to learn. I would add, however, that learning in this field is a painful and also a slow process.

I'm aware that this has been rather heavy stuff. But if I didn't arrive at a more transparent concept, it is not only (*not* only!) my fault. The problems themselves are very complicated – indeed worthwhile a whole symposium. Thus, my modest hope is that you may summarize this lecture as students do ironically after our seminars: *We are still confused, but on a higher level.*

Communication in Multicultural Settings: Resources and Strategies for Affiliation and Identity

Barbara Johnstone

Introduction

Twenty years ago, communication between people who were different in certain ways was called „cross-cultural communication". Somewhat the same thing is now more usually called „intercultural communication". These two strands of research flow out of each other and their practitioners don't usually think of them as contrasting. But they are based in some important ways on different ideas about what kinds of speakers and communicative situations are the norm. I'd like to begin by tracing the differences between the two ways of imagining communication and otherness that I think are implied in research on „cross-cultural" and „intercultural" communication. I'll suggest that each is based on a different notion of the relationships between nations, cultures, and people, as well as on different assumptions about the default situations in which nations, cultures, and people meet. Then I would like to sketch the emergence of a third approach, one which might label the phenomena in question „multicultural communication".

Multicultural communication, I will suggest, is increasingly the norm in the relatively heterogeneous, unfocussed, multiethnic, polyglot conditions that characterize the social worlds of more and more people everywhere. These are situations in which nations and cultures, or people and cultures, are not in one-to-one correspondence, but instead individuals draw on social and linguistic resources from many cultures. As a result, different ways of acting and taking meet within individuals rather than at social boundaries or within social groups. Work that sees communication among people who are different as „multicultural" argues for a less deterministic view of the relationship between culture and linguistic behavior than is suggested in the frameworks of cross-cultural or intercultural communication.

In the process of sketching these three approaches, I'll summarize a number of studies, by me and by others. At the end, I will briefly explore two metaphors for what happens when languages and cultures meet in individuals: the metaphor

of crossing suggested by sociolinguist Ben Rampton, and the metaphor of border-
lands/fronteras suggested by Chicana writer Gloria Anzaldua.
    I should stress two things before I go into more detail. First, because I am a
linguist, I will focus mainly on ideas about communication and culture that
have to do with language. But I do not mean to be claiming that language is all
there is to intercultural communication. Other papers presented at this conference, by anthropologists, political scientists, communication professionals, and
others abundantly illustrated some of the other factors that influence whether
and how different people get along. Second, although I do mean to argue for
the usefulness of distinguishing three perspectives that I will call *cross-cultural,
intercultural, and multicultural*, I do not mean to be arguing for these particular
ways of defining the terms cross-cultural, intercultural, and multicultural. These
terms have been used in a variety of ways for a variety of reasons. Many people
whose work would fit best into my „crosscultural" framework identify it as
work on „intercultural" communication; the term „multicultural" has come, at
least in the U.S., to have political connotations that are not necessarily implied
in my use of the term. What I am trying to do is to describe three ways of
thinking that I think can be distinguished no matter what each is called.
    The material in the sections that follow is summarized in Table 1.

CROSS-CULTURAL	INTERCULTURAL	MULTICULTURAL
1 nation - 1 culture - 1 language	1 group - 1 culture - 1 „native" language	1 person - multiple cultures/languages
cultures/languages meet at political boundaries	cultures/languages meet at social boundaries	cultures/languages meet in individuals
explanatory concepts: *national lang.	explanatory concepts *native lang.	explanatory concepts: *linguistic resources
*bilingualism: „dual coding", „code-switching"	*bilingualism	*„heteroglossia"
*„culture shock"	*biculturalism	*„focussing" and „diffusion"
*„foreign" language teaching	*„second" language teaching	*„minority" vs. „standard" lg.; „language for special purposes"
*communication vs. non-communication	*communication vs. miscommunication	*communication always partial
Examples: Kaplan 1966, Johnstone 1986	Examples: Gumperz 1982, Scollon & Scollon 1981	Examples: Rampton 1995, Johnstone & Bean 1997

Table 1: Summary of three approaches to communication and otherness

The „Cross-cultural" communication perspective

Research undertaken from what I will call the „cross-cultural" communication perspective is based (explicitly or not) on a set of assumptions about languages and speakers and boundaries that will seem familiar to people my age or older. It's the set of unstated beliefs I grew up with. Research in this paradigm is often based on the theoretical assumption that the typical situation is one in which one nation corresponds to one culture (a nation's culture is sometimes referred to as its „national character") and that one culture corresponds to one language. The best described situation in this framework is the situation of the European monolingual nationstate, founded on principles of nationalism developed in the nineteenth century. (In nineteenth-century nationalistic theory, shared language and shared culture were two of the „pillars" on which nations were ideally perched.) Within a nation of this sort, what suits one suits all, and the nation-based linguistics on which „cross-cultural" research is based pays scant attention to variation within national traditions (except for variation between „correct" and „incorrect" forms). Cultures meet, in this framework of thought, at political boundaries, which are also boundaries between distinct cultural groups.

Explanatory concepts that work well in this framework include the idea of a „national language", which is assumed to correspond to the „native language" of a nation's citizens. Being able to use more than one language is associated with belonging to more than one political group, and, just as they might have dual citizenship, bilinguals might rely on dual coding in the brain, their two languages being mentally separate and chosen mainly according to where they found themselves geographically. Moving from one language to another is referred to as „switching", a metaphor that suggests an abrupt change of state. When a person went to a new country, he or she would experience „culture shock" as a result of the abrupt immersion in an incompatible system.

In the „cross-cultural" framework, language education is FLT, foreign language teaching. If you learn another language, you are able to communicate across linguistic and cultural boundaries; if you don't know the other language, you don't communicate. Intermediate forms and levels of international and interlinguistic communication do not figure clearly in the idealization.

In this framework, the best described situation would be contact between people who are very different: a Japanese and an American, for example. The most obvious situations in which cross-cultural communication would occur, hence the situations that are most likely to be studied, would involve, for example, foreign students and their native-speaking hosts, or business people from different countries. Recent work in this framework includes, for example, special issues of the journals *Language Sciences* (1996, Vol. 18 nos. 1-4 on „Contrastive Semantics and Pragmaticsn) and in *Text* (1995, Vol. 15 no. 4 on „Intercultural Discourse in Business and Technology").

Let me give two examples of research that I think is based on this set of assumptions. (Note again that not everyone uses the terms „cross-cultural" and „intercultural" the way I am using them in this essay.) The first is a paper by Robert Kaplan called „Cultural thought patterns in intercultural education" that was published in 1966. This study has been very influential, particularly in educational circles. This is partly because Kaplan gives an easy-to-remember explanation for a phenomenon that every foreign language teacher has noticed: students don't just have grammatical problems, they also have discourse-level problems, particularly in writing. Papers that are correctly spelled and that parse completely sometimes still don't work, because their structure is problematic on a more global level. Kaplan attributes this phenomenon to differences among cultures in processes of thought: „... each language and each culture has a paragraph order unique to itself, and ... part of the learning of a particular language is the mastering of its logical system" (p. 14). While English speakers, Kaplan says, think and write in the straight-line pattern represented on the left-hand side of the diagram reproduced as Figure 1, the thought and paragraph patterns of other language groups have other shapes. Semitic thinking and writing involves parallelism, for example; writers of Romance languages digress often.

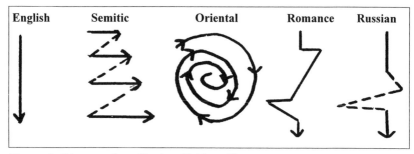

Figure 1: Diagram from Kaplan 1966, p. 15

One problem with this is that Kaplan confuses thinking with writing. If we wrote exactly the way we think, writing would be a great deal easier than it is. And of course „digress" is a rather loaded term – from what do Romance speakers supposedly „digress" except the straight line of English? It's no great coincidence, I think, that Kaplan's own system is the straight, direct, effective one.

Though, to be fair, Kaplan does stress that he is not criticizing other languages' paragraph structures, it is difficult, given his theoretical framework, to remember this. If cultures and languages are assumed to be fundamentally different, not similar, and if the boundaries between linguistic and cultural systems are seen as sources of potential conflict rather than potential creativity, then these kinds of problems are almost bound to occur.

I thought it was fair, or at least not too unfair, to single out Kaplan's paper for some criticism, because it has had so much influence; my sniping at it obviously hasn't hurt Kaplan's career. But to be even fairer I have decided to use some work of my own as a second way to highlight what the cross-cultural approach does and what it fails to do. This is a paper I wrote a decade ago called „Arguments with Khomeini: Rhetorical situation and persuasive style in crosscultural perspective" (Johnstone 1986).

More often than not, studies of cross-cultural communication arise from observations of cross-cultural miscommunication. My study was no exception; it had as its starting point an extreme example of what can go wrong when two people with very different epistemologies and norms for communicative behavior, as well as apparently clashing personalities, attempt to use language to change each other's minds. The result was crude verbal violence and complete failure to communicate. In 1979, the Italian journalist Oriana Fallaci was granted an interview with Iran's Ayatollah Khomeini. The interview turned into an abusive argument during which Fallaci stripped off the chador she was wearing, and Khomeini eventually ended it by throwing Fallaci out. In the paper, I examine the text of the interview to see what went wrong, and I propose explanations on two levels. The first is the level of strategies of logical argumentation: Khomeini repeatedly made explicit the ultimate logical grounding for his arguments – the reason on which all other reasons are based: „Islam is superior". This strategy sounds odd to Western ears. (Fallaci never said „Democracy is superior", though this belief clearly underlay most of her arguments). Furthermore, the strategy of stating and restating one's deepest beliefs is unlikely to work in a situation in which people don't share fundamental beliefs; it is a religious revival meeting strategy, not one (to Westerners) for contentious political debate.

Khomeini and Fallaci also made different choices of overall persuasive style. Fallaci presented logical arguments; Khomeini used analogical persuasive strategies like example and parable. I discussed cultural reasons for Khomeini's and Fallaci's predisposition to use different rhetorical strategies on both levels.

I tried to stress in the paper that rhetorical strategies emerge in particular situations and that interlocutors communicating in good faith can adapt to one another's styles. But it was difficult, given the assumptions about culture and communication I started with, to do justice to the fact that both interlocutors could have made other choices than they did. This was particularly true in Khomeini's case: he had spent many years in Paris and knew, or could have tried to figure out, what Fallaci was doing. My assumption that each person had just one basic way of acting and talking led me to look for and at clashes like this one rather than at the far more common situations in which people who are different (as any two people are) do manage to communicate.

This is more generally true, I think, of work in the „cross-cultural" framework. Work in this framework has trouble incorporating several kinds of things. For one thing, it makes it difficult to talk about the fact that many people can use language in more than one way. Research in the one-person-one-culture mold also doesn't provide an easy way of dealing with how people learn new patterns of communication, or how patterns change. For example, some Arabs do learn to write in native-sounding English without in the process becoming schizophrenic. And Arabic expository prose has changed in the last several decades, so that now the traditional parallelistic, poetic style schematically depicted in Kaplan's diagram is less and less common. Furthermore, research in this mold makes it difficult to see individuals who do not behave in the way they are expected to on the basis of their language or their culture. And, of course, work that is based on the one-nation-one-language idealization tends not to be about the majority of the nations and individuals in the world, who are not monolingual or monocultural.

The „Intercultural" communication perspective

People who take what I'm calling an „intercultural" perspective on communication across boundaries assume that the default situation is one in which one social group rather than one nation corresponds to one culture and to one native language or way of using language. This partly reflects the increasing 20th-century recognition, in many Western nations, of „minority groups" with civil rights, as well the increasing social integration among ethnic groupings (at least in public arenas), which has given rise in some places to more frequent interethnic contact. It is also related to people's increasing awareness of and pride in non-dominant affiliations.

In this framework, individuals' worlds are seen as defined primarily by their native language or native way of using language and by their native cultural socialization. „Cultures" are no longer associated mainly with nations, but now sometimes with ethnic groups, races, genders, sexual orientations, or even socioeconomic status, as in „the culture of poverty". The major social boundaries are boundaries between group identities rather than national boundaries. Languages and cultures meet, then, at the boundaries between distinct social groups that interact in limited circumstances. People's behavior, and their interpretations of others' behavior, is seen as made inevitable by social facts about them.

Explanatory concepts that work well in this framework include the idea of „native" language and „native" culture, the first sources of socialization which are dominant throughout one's life and in any situation. „Bidialectalism" supplements bilingualism as a possibility. It's still seen as involving „code-switching" and may not always include mastery of both „discourse systems." Biculturalism is, in this way of thinking, now possible to imagine within a nation and sometimes encouraged (especially for subordinate „minority" groups).

Language teaching is easiest seen in this framework as SLT: „second"-language teaching, since second languages are not necessarily foreign ones. Language education may include or comprise sensitivity training to other ways of using language even when one already knows the grammar, since speakers of the same language may have different ways of using it. The possibilities are not, then, either communication or non-communication, since *mis*communication (that is, communication that fails only in one key way) can be the result of contact among people with different native languages and/or cultures. In fact, miscommunication is often seen as the most likely result of intercultural contact.

In this framework, the best described situation would be contact between people of different cultures within a nation. The most obvious situations in which intercultural communication would occur, hence the situations people are likely to study, would be situations in which people of different cultures regularly interacted in public. In many cases the two groups share a language; the differences that tend to be scrutinized are differences in how the language is used and interpreted: in how people speak and when and what they mean by what they say.

One example of research in this framework is summarized in an anecdote which I quote at length from John Gumperz' (1982) well-known work on „discourse strategies":

> *In a staff cafeteria at a major British airport, newly hired Indian and Pakistani women were perceived as surly and uncooperative by their supervisor as well as by the cargo handlers whom they served. Observation revealed that while relatively few words were exchanged, the intonation and manner in which these words were pronounced were interpreted negatively. For example, when a cargo handler who had chosen meat was asked whether he wanted gravy, a British assistant would*

say „ Gravy?" using rising intonation. The Indian assistants, on the other hand, would say the word using falling intonation: „Gravy." We taped relevant sequences, including interchanges like these, and asked the employees to paraphrase what was meant in each case. At first the Indian workers saw no difference. However, the English teacher and the cafeteria supervisor could point out that „Gravy", said with a falling intonation, is likely to be interpreted as 'This is gravy', i.e. not interpreted as an offer but rather as a statement, which in the context seems redundant and consequently rude. When the Indian women heard this, they began to understand the reactions they had been getting all along which had until then seemed incomprehensible. They then spontaneously recalled intonation patterns which had seemed strange to them when spoken by native English speakers. At the same time, supervisors learned that the Indian women's falling intonation was their normal way of asking questions in that situation, and that no rudeness or indifference was intended. (p. 173)

The social boundary here is between ethnic groups and the linguistic boundary between ways of using and interpreting English. Like most work on intercultural communication, it is a study of miscommunication between two groups which are also segregated in other ways (economically or socially) and who talk to each other only for a limited set of reasons.

Ron and Suzanne Scollon's work on intercultural communication in Alaska is also well known. In „Athabaskan-English Interethnic Communication" (1981) they diagnose miscommunications that occur in situations created by „legal and economic pressures" that „have made many individuals feel that it is necessary in pursuit of their own best interests for them to engage in communicaton with members of other ethnic groups" (11). Among these are, for example, job interviews, usually involving Athabaskan applicants and Anglo supervisors. Differences in what Scollon and Scollon call „communicative patterns" create problems in the interviews, even though the Athabaskans speak English (and in fact may not speak any Athabaskan language). Scollon and Scollon examine how Anglos and Athbaskans present themselves to others (Anglos feel that talk is appropriate at the beginning of a new relationship, as a way to get to know a person, whereas Athabaskans prefer to wait to talk until their interlocutors are already familiar). They also examine how Athabaskans and Anglos express social dominance and subordination (Anglo subordinates are the ones expected to be the performers, whereas Athabaskan superiors are the performers). They describe differences in the distribution of talk:

Athabaskans pause for longer between sentences than Anglos expect them to, for example, so Anglos end up unintentionally interrupting and grabbing the floor. Athabaskans are uncomfortable with leave-taking formulas that refer to the future, feeling that talking about the future is a way of courting the evil eye, so they say nothing at the ends of interactions.

Differences like these result in ethnic stereotyping, as Athabaskans decide that all Anglos talk too much, show off too much, and interrupt too much, and as Anglos decide that Athabaskans (like the Pakistani cafeteria employees) are surly and uncooperative.

Scollon and Scollon argue for a sort of sensitivity training to encourage people from each group to see the other's behavior as the result of differing communicative patterns rather than intentional rudeness. But they are hesitant to recommend that anyone adopt anyone else's ways of talking, and skeptical that that would even be possible. The chapter ends with a section entitled „A Caution About Change" in which Scollon and Scollon claim that changing a person's discourse patterns means changing a person's identity: „If someone says that an English speaker should be less talkative, less self-assertive, less interested in the future, he is saying at the same time that he should become a different person" (p. 37). Change is, in general, difficult to deal with in the framework of intercultural communication, since people's behavior is seen as determined by their culture and language.

Work in this framework also has trouble incorporating individuals who can act in more than one way, and people who act in ways that are not predicted on the basis of their culture and language. This model of communication sees people as highly constrained by cultural socialization, so it also tends to make it hard to notice the ways in which people's choices can be strategic, consciously or unconsciously: how communicative patterns can be adapted to situation and interlocutors rather than automatic. Furthermore, it is not easy in this model to account for fragmentary, incomplete knowledge of one's „native" language and/ or culture, like that of many Athabaskans, for that matter (Charley Basham, personal communicadon), or to account for the fact that most speakers have more or less expertise in several ways of acting, talking, and being. As Florian Coulmas (1981) and others have pointed out, the concept of the „native" speaker is not unproblematic. It is also frustratingly difficult, in „intercultural" communication research, to see exactly how people *could* ever get along successfully across boundaries. Sensitivity training notwithstanding, if people's early cultural and linguistic socialization forces them to act in certain ways and not others, and if to adopt new communcative strategies or expectations is to change one's personality, then adaptation seems utopian.

The „Multicultural" communication perspective

In what I will call the „multicultural communication" framework, an individual is seen as potentially having access to multiple cultures, multiple ways of using language. The normal situations, in this framework, are multi-ethnic, polyglot ones that involve communication at and across social and linguistic boundaries, and the normal speakers are ones with multiple competences. Language is seen as the result of choices from among resources provided by multiple models, choices which can be strategic (rhetorical) or expressive of self. Cultures and languages meet, then, within individuals, who group themselves and are grouped by others, for various and changing purposes, into various social groups.

Explanatory concepts that work well in this framework include the idea of linguistic resources (rather than „native" and „second" languages or varieties), the idea, that is, that at least some people may not have one strongly dominant way of being, acting, or talking, but might instead regularly draw on multiple cultures and languages. Bakhtin's (1980) concept of „heteroglossia" also works well in this framework of ideas, as do approaches to multilingualism that stress „code-mixing" and the possibility of a range of kinds and levels of multiple language use (see, for example, Gardner-Chloros 1995). Rather than seeing cultures and languages as monolithic wholes of which one could either have one (and be monolingual and/or monocultural) or two (and be bicultural and/or bilingual), this approach makes it possible to think in terms of relative cultural and linguistic „focussing" and „diffusion" (LePage and Tabouret-Keller 1985): beliefs and ways of talking are sometimes, for some purposes, widely shared, and sometimes relatively idiosyncratic and variable. Discourse in the multicultural mode tends to be not as much about „native languages" or „second languages" as about varieties used in different contexts: „home languages", „school languages", „standard languages". In this context, in which non-standard varieties are taken more seriously, discussion of processes and politics of standardization (and of resistance to standardization) become more likely. Language teaching is now seen increasingly as LSP: languages for „special purposes" such as commerce or academia (even the most tradidonal „foreign" languages in the U.S., French and German, are now offered more and more often in specialized sections like „German for business" or „French reading), and it becomes possible to envision language learners as people who take a Peircian stance of „thirdness", adopting some aspects of enculturation, resisting others, creating a sort of „inter-culture" as they create „interlanguage" (Kramsch 1993). Communication across boundaries is always partial, from the multicultural perspective, since no two people control or use exactly the same set of resources.

In this framework, the best described situation would be speech among people who have multiple resources to draw on: people exposed to multicultural settings (often, though by no means exclusively, „minority group" members), to the media; people who live or work at social boundaries. The most obvious situations in which multicultural communication would occur, hence the situations people are likely to study, would be, for example, public speech, or speech in public institutions that mix people from various areas or groups (such as schools).

Let me give two examples of research in this framework. The first, which I'll summarize only extremely briefly, is the work of Ben Rampton (1985) in England. Rampton has been studying adolescents in two multiethnic neighborhoods where children of Caribbean Black ancestry, East Asians, and white Anglos mingle and compete in school and in youth clubs. His interest is in what he calls „crossing", or the use of language varieties associated with ethnic groups other than one's own – for example, the use of Caribbean Creole-sounding speech by Asians and whites or of Panjabi by whites or Afro-Caribbeans. He finds that crossing occurs at moments when social relationships are in question, „when the ordered flow of habitual social life [is] loosened" (p. 281), often at the boundaries of expected routines. Crossing serves sometimes to challenge expected relationships, as when adolescents use Indian-sounding English in somewhat playful resistance to teachers, and it is used in games, in music, in interaction across sexes. Making use, however briefly and occasionally, of linguistic resources associated with other groups allows these adolescents to construct „a new inheritance from within multiracial interaction itself" (p. 297).

Rather than focussing on communication (or, more usually, miscommunication) *across* boundaries, Rampton focusses on communication *at* the boundaries. This is what I've also begun to do, in a different way, in the work I'm doing, with Judith Bean, in Texas, which I'd now like to talk about briefly.

Both outsiders and Texans tend to think that there is a single linguistic model towards which all Texans either aim or decide not to aim: something called „Texas speech" or „talking Texan". Texans' sense of linguistic unity and uniqueness is part of a more general sense, rooted in history and now encouraged in education and commerce, that Texas is special, bigger and better and different than any other state. (Or any other country, for that matter.) But even the most casual observation shows that not all Texans speak alike, nor do all share the same norms for speech. There are many very different resources available in Texas for the creation and display of idiosyncratic ways of being and sounding, and the many Texans who interact with people outside their immediate communities, either privately or in more public media, have access to varying sets of these resources. Texas is a particularly suitable locale for a study of the of these resources. Texas is a particularly suitable locale for a study of the linguistic effects of multiple cultural models. To varying degrees, people in Texas speak English like southerners, like Californians, like midwesterners; they speak Spanish, Tex-Mex, Vietnamese, German, Czech; they use features of African-American English Vernacular and traditions of African-American oratory; they project colorful, direct western personalities or genteel, indirect southern ones. Texans shape languages to use as they shape individual identities in the „multidimensional social space" (LePage and Tabouret-Keller 1985) suggested by these and other possibilities.

Not all linguistic possibilities are open to all Texans: not all speak Spanish equally well, for example, and some are only able to make small symbolic stabs at sounding Southern. Some Texans do continue to live in tightly focused communities in which linguistic resources are limited and homogeneity is accordingly high. We are not trying to undo the results of dialectology based in such communities, but rather to extend the study of linguistic variation so that it provides a model of the language of people in other, more public contexts as well.

We are interested in a setting in which there are multiple models for how to talk and in educated, mobile, middle-class people (not unlike ourselves) whose social ties to one another and to some of the people they seek to influence are public rather than private (and who accordingly frequently employ public modes of discourse such as speech-making, teaching, publishing, recording, and so on). In such settings, we think, linguistic variation can best be understood as the result of individuals' creation of distinct voices that express changeable, idiosyncratic identities. We think that this process involves individual speakers' selection and combination of resources provided by the regional and social models available to them.

To give you just one brief example of how this can work, let's look at an excerpt from a newspaper column by Molly Ivins. Ivins is a political commentator and humorist who is well known throughout the United States. She is a liberal writing about a very conservative state, thus both an outsider and an insider in Texas, and her audience includes both Texans and non-Texans, people who agree with her and people who violently disagree. She manages the competing demands by shifting apparently effortlessly between a way of talking that is almost stereotypically Texan and a way of talking that is almost stereotypically standard, creating a very distinctive voice in the process. Ivins' stereotypical Texas speech makes fun of stereotypical Texans, but it also identifies her as a Texan. She shifts in and out of her West Texas voice between clauses and within them, using it, sometimes in humor, sometimes for ironic criticism, to express her regional and individual identity. Shifts away from her Texas voice tend to be into very formal, elevated standard language that marks her as educated and cosmopolitan. Ivins' voice is even more heterogeneous, however: she also expresses in her speech her *rejection* of another of the possible models for the action and speech of a white female Texan, that of the delicate, dependent Southern belle (the sort of woman you might be familiar with from *Gone With the Wind*). Ivins' discourse allows us to examine the interplay of regional, national, and individual identities and the strategic use of regional identification for rhetorical ends.

In the excerpt we will examine (from Ivins 1991), Ivins describes a debate over a Texas redistricting bill. She writes that in 1971, State Representative Guy Floyd of San Antonio:

> *a good ol' boy who had been shafted by the bill, rose to remonstrate with the chairman of the Redistricting Committee .... „Lookahere, Dell-win, " said Floyd, much aggrieved, „look at this district here. You've got a great big ball at the one end, and then a little bitty ol' strip a' land goes for about 300 miles, and then a great big ol' ball at the other end. It looks like a dumbbell. Now the courts say the districts have to be com-pact and con-tiguous. Is that your idea a' com-pact and con-tiguous? " Delwin Jones meditated at some length before replying, „Whaell, in a artistic sense, it is. " (p. 15)*

Ivins represents widely-held stereotypes of Texas speech here. She creates a laconic pace with the discourse markers *whaell, lookahere*, and *now* at the beginnings of sentences and with the long pause she describes („Delwin Jones meditated at some length"). The nonstandard South Midland phonology that characterizes Texas speech is represented by „eye-dialect" (*ol, a*) and the expressions *great big ol'* and *little bitty ol'*, and South Midland morphophonology is represented by *a artistic*.

In framing the story, Ivins' narratorial voice is sometimes depicted as using standard, even elevated, speech. However, even here Ivins shifts styles. For example, she begins the redistricting story with colloquial phrasing: „a good ol' boy who had been shafted by the bill," then switches to more formal diction in the verb phrase, „rose to remonstrate with the chairman of the Redistricting Committee". She goes on to identify him as a man „much aggrieved". Through formal lexical choices such as *remonstrate* and *aggrieved*, Ivins makes an implicit claim to the intellectual authority of outside observer and critic. Through phrasing such as „good ol' boy" she invokes and satirizes a regional stereotype, at the same time displaying her identity with it through her fluency in it.

What Molly Ivins calls „speaking Texan" has a more personal function as well: displaying the public freedom of expression and forthrightness sometimes denied the traditional Southern woman. Ihrough her linguistic choices, Ivins simultaneously asserts her toughness and her sense of play. Linguistic resources associated with region (the west) and gender (maleness) give Ivins a way of emphasizing her convictions; the resources of class and nation (standard English) give her a means of grounding her intellectual analysis. Together, Ivins' choices from and juxtapositions of the resources available to her allow her to establish a clearly individual discourse style with which to express a clearly individual identity.

Two metaphors

Now that I've illustrated, I hope, what I mean by the „multicultural" perspective on communication, let me end by talking briefly about two metaphors that have been used in connection with this way of thinking. Ben Rampton's metaphor for one thing that can go on at communicative borders is „crossing". This metaphor seems to me particularly apt for the ways people can/do occasionally and strategically borrow from other groups and people. Like „cross-dressing," it suggests something that is at least a slight aberration. (Note that I'm not claiming that Rampton's work presents „crossing" as an aberration, just that the metaphor of crossing itself tends to suggest that.) Still, it's a useful way of talking: people can cross boundaries, which is something we haven't been very good at modelling until recently.

Crossing is also the metaphor used by anthropologist Dan Rose (1990) in his critique of „bureaucratic" ethnography. Rose urges ethnographers to experiment not only with new forms of representation (new ways of writing ethnography) but with new ways of doing etnography that explore boundaries and create „reversals" via what Rose calls „ethnographic poetics". Ethnography, he says, should be more like postcolonial literature. As Rose puts it:

> An ethnographic poetics desires more, indeed nothing less than to inhabit a zone of contact (by crossing over it again and again) which cannot be defined but must be explored, which can take its shape through ethnography, poetry, fiction, and the other arts (...). (p. 45)

Another metaphor for communication at boundaries is suggested by Gloria Anzaldua, the author of *Borderlands/La Frontera* (1987). Anzaldua is a writer (not a linguist but very savvy about language) who comes from „the valley": the part of Texas that is on the Rio Grande border with Mexico. She calls herself a „Chicana", one of many terms people like her choose among depending on what they want to stress (or not) about themselves at the moment. Here is her description of what goes on at the linguistic borderland:

> *For a people who are neither Spanish nor live in a country in which*
> *Spanish is the first language; for a people who live in a country in which*
> *English is the reigning tongue but who are not Anglo; for a people who*
> *cannot entirely identify with either standard (formal, Castillian) Spanish*
> *nor standard English, what recourse is left to them but to create their*
> *own language? A language which they can connect their identity to, one*
> *capable of communicating the realities and values true to themselves – a*
> *language with terms that are neither espanol ni ingles, but both. We speak*
> *a patois, a forked tongue, a variation of two languages.* (p. 55)

This suggests a scenario in which things are more routinely mixed, a landscape of bilingual signs, license plates from another state or country, houses and people that look as if they could be on the other side, people picking and choosing from among various ways of talking and being.

This metaphor seems apt in my part of the world, where it comes from, the borderlands between Anglo North America and Hispanic Central and South America. People are metaphorically as well as physically close to the border in Texas. Where I live, and maybe more and more everywhere, it seems to me important to study linguistic borderlands, because communication is, more and more, multicultural in addition to being cross-cultural or intercultural.

References

Anzaldua, Gloria. 1987. *Borderlands/La Frontera; The New Mestiza.* San Francisco: Aunt Lute Book Co.

Bakhtin, Mikhail M. 1980 [1935]. *The dialogic imagination.* Austin: University of Texas Press.

Coulmas, Florian, ed. 1981. *Festschrift for Native Speaker.* The Hague: Mouton.

Gardner-Chloros, Penelope. 1995. Code-switching in Community, Regional and National Repertoires: The Myth of the Discreteness of Linguistic Systems. *One Speaker. Two Languages: Cross-Disciplinary Perspectives on Code-Switching,* ed. by Lesley Milroy and Pieter Muysken, 68-89. Cambridge, UK: Cambridge UP.

Gumperz, John J. 1982. Interethnic Communication. Chapter 8 of *Discourse Strategies.* Cambridge: Cambridge University Press.

Ivins, Molly. 1991. *Molly Ivins Can't Say That, Can She?* New York: Random House.

Jaszczolt, Katarzyna and Ken Turner, guest eds. 1996. Contrastive Semantics and Pragmatics, 2 vols. Vol 18, Nos. 14 of *Language Sciences.*

Johnstone, Barbara. 1986. Arguments with Khomeini: Rhetorical Situation and Persuasive Style in Cross-Cultural Perspective, *Text* 6(2), 171-187.

Johnstone, Barbara. 1996. *The Linguistic Individual: Self-expression in Language and Linguistics.* New York: Oxford UP.

Johnstone, Barbara and Judith Mattson Bean. 1997. Self-Expression and Linguistic Variation. *Language in Society*

Kaplan, Robert. 1966. Cultural thought patterns in intercultural education. *Language learning*, 16, 1-20.

Kramsch, Claire. 1993. *Context and culture in language teaching.* Oxford: Oxford UP.

LePage, R. B. and Andree Tabouret-Keller. 1985. *Acts of Identity: Creole-Based Approaches to Language and Ethnicity.* Cambridge UP.

Rampton, Ben. 1995. *Crossing: Language and Ethnicity Among Adolescents.* London: Longman.

Rose, Dan. 1990. *Living the ethnographic life.* Newbury Park, Calif. Sage.

Scollon, Ron and Suzanne B.K. Scollon. 1981. Athabaskan-English Interethnic Communication. Chapter 2 of *Narrative. Literacy and Face in Interethnic Communication.* Norwood, N.J.: Ablex.

Ulijn, Jan M. and Denise E. Murray, eds. 1995. Intercultural Discourse in Business and Technology. Vol 15, no. 4 of *Text.*

Thirdness: The Intercultural Stance

Claire Kramsch

Introduction

The notion of „communicative competence" seems to have been now supplemented or even replaced in Europe by a type of language competence that takes into account differences in „culture" among interlocutors from different language groups. Two adjectives are used to qualify this new type of competence: „intercultural" usually refers to communication across national divides, „cross-cultural" is used to characterize communication across race, class, gender, ethnicity lines. These two terms reflect a common concern with communication among people who may not share a common language nor a common history, place in society, attitudes and worldviews, and who may imagine the future differently. The switch of adjective and the phonological analogy between communicative competence and intercultural competence seem to suggest that the latter is but a variant, a necessary outcome of, or a more refined version of a general ability to communicate with other fellow human beings. But is that really the case? Do they both share the same theoretical underpinnings? what is the nature and scope, the objectives of intercultural competence?

I propose first to briefly review the relationship of communicative competence and intercultural competence. I then briefly outline a theoretical framework for exploring language competence across cultures. This framework is then used for analyzing a case study of an encounter between speakers from different cultures.

Communicative Competence Revisited

In the mind of Dell Hymes, the anthropologist who coined the term 30 years ago in 1966, communicative competence had a distinct flavor of both social and cultural relativity. From his study of various Indian cultures and as can be seen in his early model of an ethnography of speaking, Hymes knew well how problematic it was to study linguistic and cultural competence separately. He writes:

> *The solution would be to take speech itself as an object of study, as having patterning of its own, requiring both linguistic and social analysis. It would*

41

be recognized that communities differ in the patterning their histories have given to speech, the place speech has in their repertoires of communicative mode and symbolic form, the kinds of ability associated with speech that are encouraged and discouraged, their allocation across genders, ages, statuses and roles. There continues to be need for a comprehensive conception of the abilities associated with language. This is especially clear in connection with the teaching and learning of language and in connection with differences among groups. (1987:219)

This statement gives a good idea of what constituted communicative competence for Hymes: a recognition and understanding of social differences in the use of language, an understanding of a social group's history, its forms of symbolic capital, its social structure, and of the distribution of power as reflected in its use of language. It included the „tacit knowledge" described by Boas, Sapir, Polanyi, i.e., an understanding of the norms of interaction and interpretation of a given speech community, its totems and taboos, its „members' resources (Fairclough 1992), its differential distribution of abilities, of rights to speak and to be listened to. Therefore, concludes Hymes,

[A general theory of communicative competence] will not be able to specify absolutely and in advance the character of communicative competence for a particular case, for that will be relative to the persons, activities and needs involved, and perhaps, to judgments that have an ethical and political dimension...The value of the concept...is in part that of a comprehensive, regulative, heuristic guide. (ibidem p. 226)

As we know, however, in language education, it was linguistics, not anthropology that carried the day, combined with an individualistic, positivistic view of the communication process as exchange of information. This view was infused with a Western ideology, based on the enlightened belief in the democratizing value of symmetrical, unlimited turns-at-talk between like-minded speakers and hearers in free information exchanges, irrespective of their cultural backgrounds. Communicative competence became measurable against the politically free speech conditions available to native speakers.

However, as Bourdieu said, „c'est une illusion de croire que le marché communicatif est soumis exclusivement au principe de la maximisation du rendement informatif" (Bourdieu 1982:44). As Mary Pratt remarks, it is a utopia to believe that cross-cultural communication occurs in clearly identifiable and universally agreed upon speech situations, through measurable levels of individual linguistic proficiency, and with the help of teachable communicative strategies and tactics (Pratt 1987). Recent studies of multilingual/multicultural discourse communities in Central or Latin America have shown the very complex ways in which language construct cultural identities (Le Page and Tabouret-Keller 1985).

There have been recent proposals to operationalize the various components of an *intercultural competence* in foreign language education. Noteworthy are the influential proposals made by language educators like Howard Nostrand in the US or by Michael Byram and Geneviève Zarate in Europe. These proposals emphasize the need to understand the Other on his/her own terms, and claim to relate the Other to the Self in a dialectic moment of self- and other-discovery. However, these proposals have, in my view, the limitations of structuralist approaches:

- they see the boundaries between cultures, between Self and Other, Native and Foreign, as much more *rigid* than they really are.
- they see cultures as much more *homogeneous* than they really are, especially in national terms.
- they see cultures as much more *equal/symmetrical* than they really are. Although they have acknowledged conflict in an anthropological sense as inherent in the apperception of the Other, they have not dealt with conflictual issues of legitimation, power and the politics of recognition between minority and dominant cultures. Cross-cultural communication has mostly been viewed as a „problem-to be solved", a struggle on the way to reaching consensus through rational talk between rationally-minded adults. Yet, as we know, consensus might not be possible, or, indeed, desirable, if there is no commensurable ground between members of different social groups.

I propose to examine the concept of intercultural competence from a post-structuralist perspective, where social boundaries easily get blurred, cultural identities are not only bureaucratically determined but also self-ascribed, and the concept of a third space is becoming a recurring theme in writings from various disciplines.

Theories of Thirdness

The growing interest in a dialectical principle of Thirdness comes from the work of three scholars in loosely connected fields: Charles Peirce in semiotics, Mikhail Bakhtin in philosophy and literary criticism, Homi Bhabha in cultural criticism.

Peirce's Thirdness
The renewed interest in Peircean semiotics right now is a case in point (Peirce 1898/1931, Oller 1995, Hanks 1996, Sheriff 1994, Petrilli 1993, van Lier 1996

ms.). In his visionary philosophy of almost 100 years ago, Peirce distinguished between three modes of being. *Firstness* is the mode by which we apprehend reality, gain immediate consciousness of incoming bits of information, or isolated phenomena. *Secondness* is the mode by which we react to this information, and by which we act and interact with others within a social context. *Thirdness* is a relational process-oriented disposition, that is built in time through habit, and that allows us to perceive continuity in events, to identify patterns, and make generalizations. All three modes of being coexist, of course, at any given time, but only Thirdness is able to make meaning out of the other two and to build a sense of identity and permanence.

These three modes of being correspond to the three aspects of the signs that humans use to give meaning to the world around them. A sign can either be an image of its object (icon), or refer to it (index), or be a conventionalized representation of it (symbol). In Peirce's semiotic system, a sign, such as a word or an image, not only has an object to which it is related iconically, indexically, or symbolically, but it also evokes in the mind of its receiver another sign, which Peirce calls „the interpretant". It is through the interpretant that signs have meaning rather than just signification. Over time, iconic and indexical signs become reified as conventional symbols; they create paths of expectations that are shared among members of the same signifying community and that allow them to anticipate future events.

Peirce's semiotic theory can help us understand what cross-cultural communication entails. It means:

1. relating linguistic, visual, acoustic signs to other signs along paths of meaning that are shared or at least recognized as such by most socialized members of the community. To use an example that will serve our purposes in the case study below: in Germany, the sign of a clock showing five minutes before twelve *signifies* „fünf vor zwölf", but it *means* „warning" or „danger".

2. relating signs to prior signs whose meanings have accumulated through time in the imagination of the people who use them or see them used. Thus, for example, the words „Ausländer" in Germany and „foreigner" in the United States have different histories, hence different weight, value, and connotations.

3. relating signs to human intentionalities. Because signs are used for a purpose (they are „motivated"), they are intended to evoke quite specific interpretants in the minds of their recipients. Of course, given the heterogeneity of modern-day societies, they may evoke in different people other interpretants than those intended. For example, the interpretant „danger" for the

5-before-12 German sign might be lost on French or American viewers who might interpret it literally as an indication of public time.

Signs in one culture are not limited to the meanings historically given them by members of one social community. They are constantly resemioticized by outsiders who have come in, by insiders who have gone out and come into contact with other cultures, other experiences, and who now give different meaning to the traditional signs used in their original community.

Bakhtin's Triadic Dialogism

But how do we know when a sign in a foreign culture is to be read as the expression of one individual's purpose or as the collective purpose of, say, a national community, since a person can act either as an individual or as a member of a group? This is where Bakhtin's notion of dialogism helps put the focus on the third, most important element of the Self-Other dyad: namely, the fact that the one individual does not exist, has no meaning, cannot define him/herself without the other. Michael Holquist (1990) identifies the following characteristics of Bakhtin's dialogism:

1) Dialogism is a differential relation. For Bakhtin, the use of language in dialogue is the prime site in which difference – while still remaining different – can serve as the building blocks of simultaneity (both/and at the same time), because the existence of one is the very condition for the existence of the other. For example, while in Europe, I was accustomed to define myself according to the national category imposed on me by others, i.e., I was French not German or Italian. I did not generally define myself through the whiteness of my skin. Now in the United States, I have to define myself according to quite other categories, for which I have to check the appropriate box on official forms like the census, or grant application. I am obliged to think of myself as White, Caucasian, Woman, European against other ethnicities and races. Part of becoming a member of another community is precisely the process of constructing your own identity in relation to that of others. We are what others are not. We perceive the world through the time/space of the self (our two basic categories of perception), but also through the time/space of the other.

2) Dialogism is not only relation, it is always response. For Bakhtin, cultural and personal identity does not precede the encounter, but, rather, it gets constructed in language through the encounter with others. An utterance is always a response to an actual or potential utterance that preceded it. We are the role we are playing at this particular moment *in response* to the roles played by others.

„I am an event, the event of constantly responding to utterances from the different worlds I pass through. " (Holquist 1990:48)

The individual, like the sign in Peirce's system, does not exist in any other way than as *a response to a sign with other signs.*

3) Dialogism is not only a relation to the Other in space, but also to others and other manifestations of self in time. Dialogue, composed of utterances and responses, links not only present to present, but present to past and future. Within the same utterance I can at once enact my present relationship to my interlocutor, evoke past relationships and mortgage our future. More important than either the utterance or the response taken separately, is the relation between my words and prior words. Dialogism includes the third, constitutive warrant of historical change in discourse. As Michael Holquist remarks:

> *The thirdness of dialogue frees my existence from the very circumscribed meaning it has in the limited configuration of self/other relations available in the immediate time and particular place of my life. For in later times, and in other places, there will always be other configurations of such relations, and in conjunction with that other, my self will be differently understood. This degree of thirdness outside the present event insures the possibility of whatever transgredience I can achieve toward myself.*
> (ibidem, p.38)

Homi Bhabha's Third Space of Enunciation

The Indian British cultural critic Homi Bhabha has, in recent years, suggested a notion of Third Space that complements on the societal level Peirce's Thirdness and Bahktin's dialogism. Locating culture in the discursive practices of speakers and writers living in post-colonial times in complex industrialized societies, Bhabha makes important points that owe a great deal to the notion of interpretation introduced by Peirce.

1) According to Bhabha, cultural difference is built into the very condition of communication because of the necessity to interpret, not just to send and receive messages.

> *The pact of interpretation is never simply an act of communication between the I and the You designated in the statement. The production of meaning requires that these two places be mobilized in the passage through a Third Space, which represents both the general conditions of language and the*

> *specific implication of the utterance in a performative and institutional*
> *strategy of which it cannot 'in itself' be conscious.* (Bhabha 1994:36)

For Bhabha, this „third space" defines the position of the speaker of an utterance who both refers to events in the outside world and, in so doing, constitutes him/herself as subject of enunciation. This position is historically contingent, socially larger than the individual, and therefore beyond any single individual's consciousness. In other words, we cannot be conscious of our interpretive strategies at the same moment as we activate them. They are the unconsciously acquired discourse practices that speak through us and that constitute our essential cultural difference. The encounter between two cultures always entails a discontinuity in the traditionally continuous time of a person's or a nation's discourse practices. For example, a foreign national does not have the same discourse regarding his/her host nation's history as a native national. The inclusion of the foreign national's perspective makes it possible to envisage, for example, a national, anti-nationalist view of a people's history. Understanding someone from another culture requires an effort of translation from one perspective to the other, that manages to keep both in the same field of vision.

2) Cultural difference gets articulated in the „highly contradictory and ambivalent space of enunciation". We always say more than we think we do because part of the meaning of what we say is already given by our position in the social structure, by the power or powerlessness that we represent, and by the subject positions we occupy in social encounters. Because it carries with it the traces of our multiple positions in the social order, says Bhabha, the cultural space carved by our words and those of others is, in modern societies, an eminently heterogeneous, indeed contradictory and ambivalent space in which third perspectives can grow in the margins of dominant ways of seeing.

3) It is because of this heterogeneity, that ensures fluidity of signs and symbols, that cultural change is conceivable.

> *It is that Third Space, though unrepresentable in itself, which constitutes*
> *the discursive conditions of enunciationthat ensure that the meaning and*
> *symbols of culture have no primordial unity or fixity; that even the same*
> *signs can be appropriated, translated, rehistoricized and read anew.*
> (Bhabha 1994:37)

For Bhabha, the speaking subject is not only, as Bakhtin would say, „full of the voices of others", but he/she reinscribes earlier voices into her own.

Each of the three theories I just examined makes thirdness play a crucial role in cross-cultural communication. From Peirce we get the notion that meaning is constructed by putting signs in relation to other signs. From Bakhtin we get the idea that personal and cultural identity is constructed in response to self- and other-ascriptions of identity. From Homi Bhabha, we learn that the intrinsic contradictions of meaning and identity in discourse are precisely what might constitute the in-be-tween space that we call *inter-* or *cross*-cultural. Rather than think of communication as the coming together of predetermined meanings and identities, engaged in reaching commensurability or consensus, thirdness encourages us to think of communication as the relational making of signs, the responsive construction of self, and the interdependence of opposites.

Whereas the discourse of communicative competence was characterized by a distinctly pragmatic-functional vocabulary that underscored the action of a subject on an object or goal via a nomenclature of skills and strategies, the discourse of cross-cultural communication, born out of geographical migra- tions and psychological displacements within and between national communities, seems to favor a spatial/relational vocabulary. For example, Homi Bhabha talks about „interstices between cultures", Maria Lugones talks about „world- travelling" as a metaphor for „putting oneself in someone else's place", others speak of margins and subject positions, others talk of boundaries or border- lands (Anzaldua 1987), of centers and peripheries. The discourse of cross- cultural communication grows out of a much more tragic view of the world than the functional discourse of communicative competence. It has matured under often painful circumstances, in non-places or places of last resort. It high- lights difference, hybridity, transience, migration, the dangerous unreliability of language but the equal dangers of silence. It draws its strength not from some intrinsic permanent quality of the individual but from a relational stance that is able to keep contradictions within the same discursive practice because they are constitutive of that practice.

A Case Study: Ausländerfeindlichkeit in Germany

The following case study is not an example of what to do and how to do it, but an illustration of the three aspects of cross-cultural communication discussed above. I would like us to look at this inconclusive exchange from a semiotic, a dialogic and a cultural studies perspective.

At a trilingual, tricultural teacher training seminar conducted in Leipzig in summer 1993, Dieter, a West-German teacher of English, explains patiently the authentic document he would recommend for teaching German in the United

States and in France: the face of a clock showing 5' of twelve in which is inscribed a giant swastika. The meaning is: Beware of neonazis! Dieter gives a serious, moralizing weight to his words as if educating non-Germans to something he, as a German, is particularly proud of.

Dieter: [this is] a button made by the students from our
           school with the hands
           of a clock
           five minutes of..
           „Fünf vor zwölf"
           five minutes of twelve it says..which is an idiom
           in German..fünf vor zwölf..um zwölf ist alles zu
           spät
           And in the middle of that clock is a swastika
           Hakenkreuz
           that's what the students made
           a very effective .. eh .. button.
           I was asked for this button several times in the
           country and outside
           when I wore it and I gave them the address of the
           students, and this was sent to some people who
           wanted to have it..em..
           We have done that .. walk, say, during school hours
           in our neighborhood as a demonstration after Moelln,
           this was..eh..(0.5 sec.)
           I'm not..I don't mean to say that things are suffi
           cient, but it's not true thatnothing is happen
           ing..eh..
           There is one certain thing which I..I I observe,
           people in the larger cities do *not* .. speak out,
           they do *not* react, they do *not* control certain..
           eh..eh actions,
           they do *not* interfere, they do *not* make other people
           stop doing what they're doing.

At this point, Donna is about to interrupt. She is obviously containing her indignation. She then performs the containment of her indignation with the same didactic intonation as Dieter used. Her tone of voice is calm but she overenunciates as if talking to a non-English speaker.

Dieter: That's the problem that we have, people shy back,
           they go home they don't stand up

Donna: I would xxxx
Dieter: they ignore it...they turn around and go away
Donna: I would
Dieter: That is what I noticed, but on the other hand
Donna: I would never use any
         thing like that in my classroom
         it's such a negative negative situation by what
         supposedly is a free media in the United States
         .. (acc) which is a joke anyway...em
         that that would just encourage even a more negative
         stere-o-type than already exists for us.
         (acc) It would kill us.
         And I would..
         And as a matter of fact I am APPALLED by that..
         .. very honestly..
         .. by somebody wearing a b::utton that has a na::zi
         sign in the middleof it
         I am to:::tally appa:::lled by that. And..em..it
         is.. if you look at America and their Nazi movement
         it is by God certainly a lot larger than the one in
         the United States it's a lot more o::pen they're
         a lot more le::gal and I don't..I think our coun
         try in and of itself has a real di::fficult
         time... looking at what's within..
         and then to start condemning other countries..
         it really bo::thers me.
         And I don't think Germans ought to use their own..
         the..the..the past in a light like that.
         It em it has a very negative ..
         we see those Ha::kenkreuze all over the schoo::ls
         and on books already and it's something I have
         worked against.

         (1.15' of talk in English. Claire: „but for German it means „beware!‟‟
         – Ali: „I understand where she comes from. But I have a lot of Jewish
         students in my classes. It would scandalize my students and scare
         them all away") Tumult of voices

Dieter: (irritated and impatient)
         Das ist ja nun v::öllig, also hat ja dann mit unse-
         rer Wahrnehmung nicht die Bohne zu tun
Ali/
Donna: Ja! ja!

```
Dieter:        also überhaupt nicht
Tumult:        xxx
Dieter:        im Gegenteil
Tumult:        xxx
Dieter(loud): wenn ich das tra::ge
Ali:           Ja!
Dieter:        und in der Öffentlichkeit..
               dann werde ich von den Faschis::ten...
               möglicherweise zusammengeschlagen..
Tumult:        xxx
Dieter (ppp):  von den Neonazis.
```

Semiotic Perspective

Taking a semiotic perspective on the data, one can say that the conflict first arises from the totally *different interpretants* that each of the participants puts the first sign in relation with, even though each one has clearly understood that this was a warning against a resurgence of Nazi practices.

1) – Dieter, a left-wing West German social democrat and teacher of English, evidently relates the clock to the missed opportunities to stand up against the Nazis during the Third Reich, and the swastika to the Nazi Party itself. The swastika is *the* sign of the stigma indelibly attached to Germany's past. The message is clear: Nie wieder!

2) – For Donna, an American teacher of German in the US, the swastika is or has been made by the American press into a symbol of a certain demonized or tabu Germany that, as a German teacher, she may not deal with in class. For her students, the message would be equally clear: „There they go again!"

Against these two interpretations of Self and Other, we have a variety of third interpretations that allow us to appreciate the relationship between the first two in a different light.

3) – Pierre, a French teacher of English in France, instinctively puts the swastika in relation to another sign, namely what for him is stereotypical German shamelessness (see his reaction: Ils sont gonflés!").

```
Michèle:       on ne se rend peut-être pas compte, Genevieve,
               tu imagines quelqu'un  qui porte ce genre de
               badge en France?  Moi j'ai mon idée sur la
               question
Geneviève:     (silence)
```

Pierre: Moi je vous réponds. Moi, je ne comprendrais
         pas..Donc c'est un usage extremement interne. Mais
         je suis d'accord avec le danger, effectivement, si
         une télévision étrangère prend quelqu'un avec ce
         bouton-la, c'est envoyé en France, et moi en France
         je fais le contre-sens. Je ne <u>comprends</u> pas. Je ne
         vois que la swastika, et j'me dis „ils sont gonflés".

We have here an inner-French dialogue, that relates the sign to the French experience of that sign during the German occupation.

For both Donna and Pierre, the WARNING value of the clock is superseded by the TABU value of the swastika. The shock of the tabu is such that the French participants do not relate this sign, for example, to the similarly motivated French button that reads: „Touche pas a mon pote" (don't touch my buddy), with which French political activists seek to protect the rights of immigrants.

4) - Uwe and Dagmar, East German teachers of English and French respectively, are the only ones to totally identify with the authors' intention; however, they relate the sign not to the missed opportunity of resistance to Hitler, but to their own continued fight against fascism in post-war Germany.

Dagmar: Also ich kann verstehen, daß die Jugendlichen das
         Zeichen benutzt haben. . .Bisher ist das Zeichen
         eindeutig besetzt gewesen, es hat immer..die ganze
         Zeit von 1933 bis 45 hinter sich gehabt, und wir
         müssen uns damit auseinandersetzen. . .ich kann
         verstehen daß die Schüler versucht haben zu provo-
         zieren, eben auch mal es zu nutzen in einem Gegensinn,
         ja, ich kann das natürlich verstehen.
Uwe: . . . weil ich nicht die geringsten Hemmungen hätte,
         mich mit <u>meinen</u> Schülern mit Faschismus auseinander-
         zusetzen . . .

Each participant re-semioticizes Dieter's „sign" according to paths created over time in his/her own culture. These resemioticizations are often dictated not only by the need to make meaning, but by the imperative to avoid the tabuus and stigmata with which certain signs have been endowed over time. It is to these acquired or acculturated taboo or stimatized „habits of the heart" (de Tocqueville cited by Bellah et al.) that each of the participants responds, as they respond to one another.

Note that these resemioticizations are not without intrinsic contradictions, as we can see in the highly conflictual and self-divided argument made by Donna in the beginning. By teaching German in the United States, Donna is in an eminently mediating position, an intercultural position par excellence. She, like many other language teachers, has had to decide where she stands vis a vis the taboos and stigmata attached to the German language, and how to talk or not to talk about them in an American context. Her indignation reveals her personal profound ambivalence about this. Her noteworthy slip of the tongue-confusion between the United States and Germany in line 15 and the confusion in her pronominal referents in lines 14 and 16 (who is the „their" in „their Nazi movement"? the „they" in „they're a lot more legal"?) – these linguistic ambiguities may be seen as revealing not only her own difficult professional subject position, but the deep ambiguity of American discourse vis-a-vis fascism in general.

Dialogic Perspective

Looking now at the data from a dialogic perspective, one could say that the source of the conflict is indeed here a lack of understanding on the part of the participants of the *prior texts* which the others are responding to.

Ali: `I could see the headlines in the school's newspaper,`
`somebody..you know.. taking a picture of that to`
`show what the German program   is!...`

Donna: `Oh yeah`

Ali: `I'm serious!`

Dieter: `Aber dies ist eine deutsche Schule, in Deutschland,`
`in der das passiert.`
`Und ich bekenne mich dazu, daß ich die Situation`
`für gefährlicherhalte als vielleicht die Mehrheit`
`der Deutschen das tun.`
`Und deswegen trage ich das Ding.`
`Und ich unterstütze die Schüleraktion, und ich`
`vermittle die Adressen undsoweiter.`
`Das ist eine bewußte politische Aktion, und em das`
`ist..die Furcht.. vor..dem Neonazismus.`

Donna: `Aber für uns würde das genau das Gegenstück bedeuten`

Dieter: `Ja, ist ja in Ordnung (tumult of voices), das sage`
`ich doch gar nicht(tumult of voices), aber dann`
`kann man doch meine Handlung nicht damit vergleichen.`

Ali: `Aber wir vergleichen gar nicht`
`(Tumult of voices)`

Dieter: `Aber so kommt es raus`

Dieter makes it clear what he is responding to by wearing this button: besides demonstrating against the murders of Turkish immigrants in Moelln, he is displaying the citizen involvement, democratic engagement, and political activism that Germans have been reproached with lacking in the past. Indeed, he is showing the Americans and the French in the group that he is not like his German ancestors.

Donna's and Ali's prior text is the Jewish presence in the United States, for whom American neonazism has a totally different value („eine ganz andere Wahrnehmung") from Third Reich nazism, and for whom America is, by and large, *not* a candidate for self-criticism, unlike Germany. One could say that in a sense, Dieter's stigma is Donna and Ali's taboo. The more Dieter tries to shed that stigma, the more he reinforces the taboo placed on the American teachers of German, Donna and Ali. It is interesting to see how cross-cultural communication still continues to occur, despite this seeming deadlock polarity.

Dieter, who had the choice of presenting his button in German (after all the French did this in French in a previous presentation, relying on the agreed upon simultaneous translation by participants in the group), chooses to present it in English, thus showing consideration for the international community of interlocutors, who all understand English, but also instinctively presenting himself as a post-war English-speaking West-German (something that Uwe, the East-German teacher of English never does once throughout the whole seminar). Following suit, Donna responds in English, although she too could have used German, since she is a German teacher. Her use of English should not only be read as a linguistic convergence of two interlocutors – which it undoubtedly is – but also as her desire to position herself squarely as a Jewish-American voice on the subject. In addition to this linguistic convergence/divergence, we see Donna adopting the very same moralizing/didactic tone Dieter used to oppose him.

Dieter's switch from English to German shows Dieter's intense need to be understood on his own German terms. Donna and Ali, even though vehemently disagreeing with the content of his argument, switch to German too, showing at least linguistic solidarity and their desire to calm the waters and save Dieter's face. In fact, each of the participants in this exchange draws on prior discourses in their own political culture to both show solidarity with one another and to distance themselves from one another. In her counter-diatribe, Donna aligns herself with Dieter's moralistic, didactic tone, and uses the same kind of foreigner-talk style as Dieter did – a discursive tit for tat, no doubt, but nevertheless a way of showing that she takes him seriously and is, in fact, closer to him than she thinks, since she too is responding to the anti-German defamatory pressure of the American press in the same manner as Dieter is responding to the post-war defamatory pressure of international opinion on Nazi Germany. Despite their obvious angers, both are in fact quite close, as each one is desperately trying to make the other understand the taboos and stigmata under which each of them is living.

This is where the third perspective from the East German teachers proved to be invaluable. Both Dagmar and Uwe draw on yet another stock of prior discourses, namely the socialist discourse of struggle against fascism.

Dagmar:
```
Also ich kann verstehen, daß die Jugendlichen
das Zeichen benutzt haben, so wie es ist, und
daß sie es nicht gebrochen haben, denn das ist
ein Zeichen einer Provokation. . . Ich würde
sagen, dieser kleine Text, „Fünf vor Zwölf",
drei kleine Worte oder eine Zahl, würden den
Blickwinkel vielleicht ein bißchen verändern
von dem Hakenkreuz, und das kann dann also
diese andere Botschaft, eben den Gegenwert,
die Umkehrung der Werte... daß man das mitkriegt.
Vielleicht regt das einen Augenblick an..zum
Stehen-bleiben, oder zum Hingucken.
```

The terms „Provokation", „Gegenwert", „Umkehrung der Werte" belong to a GDR discourse of political activism that is related to but different from Dieter's left-wing radical discourse. Dagmar shows solidarity with the intention of Dieter's button even though her tone is quite different: no personalized experiences like those found in Dieter's and Donna's statements, no overuse of „ich"; instead, impersonal statements to the message itself and its potential impact.

Critical Theoretical Perspective

Finally, taking the perspective of critical theory, we can identify larger *social discourses* that speak through the participants in this short exchange. As we have seen, Donna speaks the American Discourse of moral tolerance and constructive, positive thinking. For her, such a button goes against the American concept of political activism where one is expected to fight FOR a cause, not through negative advertising and through instilling fear, but through positive advocacy and a positive outlook. It is Doris, the other West-German in the group, that gives an interesting third perspective on the polarity between Dieter and Donna:

Doris: Ich würde so etwas auch nicht tragen, weil ich
           glaube daß viele Leute <u>nicht</u> genau genug <u>hin</u>schauen.
           Die schauen gar nicht so auf die Uhr, sondern die
           sehen dann wirklich nur noch das Hakenkreuz, hm?
           Also ich glaub das ist schon etwas Subtiles, ich
           würde eine Werbung, ach was heißt hier Werbung, ich
           würde also gegen den Nazismus nicht mit dem Symbol
           des Nazismus direkt kämpfen.
Dieter: Ich würde es nicht so weit tabuisieren

Doris draws here on the commercial discourse of effective advertising, to which
Dieter answers in the rational discourse mode of left-wing Social Democrats –
two West-German postwar discourses. His explicit mention of taboo names the
problem quite well, in my view, and points to a problem that has not been
adequately addressed in intercultural communication research. For, it is this
level of social discourse, with its stigmata and taboos, that is the most difficult
for cross-cultural communication to deal with. Uwe gives yet another perspective
on this taboo when he says in the end in German to Claudia, the German Goethe
Institute representative in New York:

Uwe: ich habe das Gefühl, für mich jetzt, daß wir an
           einem Punkt angelangt sind [. . .] daß ein Rest an
           Fremdheit gegenüber den anderen Kulturen offen-
           sichtlich da bleibt. Weil ich nicht die geringsten
           Hemmungen hätte, mich mit <u>meinen</u> Schülern mit
           Faschismus auseinanderzusetzen, da.. von mir aus
           ... offensichtlich kann man das bei Euch nicht
           machen, das verstehe ich nicht, weil ich die Kultur
           nicht...ich muß das akzeptieren.
Claudia: ich finde genügend Programme in Amerika, wo man
           sich mit dem Nationalsozialismus auseinandersetzt,
           und wo man sich auch mit der Swastika auseinander-
           setzt
Uwe: soviel ich weiß...auch wie wir das hier tun dürfen?
Claudia: es ist eine ganze andere |Wahrnehmung
Uwe: |ja eben!

We have here an interesting German-German dialogue across two irreducible
historical and geographical frontiers, and between two incommensurable
perceptions or „Wahrnehmungen" of fascism, that of an East German living
now in a unified Germany, that of a West German living now in the United

States. These „Wahrnehmungen" have over time been either stigmatized or, indeed, made taboo, i.e., they have been pretty much removed from rational public discourse.

Along each of the dimensions explored above, the participants can be seen constructing semiotic relations, defining themselves in response to others' constructions of them, and dealing with the incommensurable discourses of others. Their delicate manoeuvers to show each other solidarity and personal investment (in the form of empathy or anger), while respecting each other's collective taboos and irreducible differences in worldviews show a willingness to continue to relate to one another, not because of a common ground, which they can have no hope of achieving given their incommensurable histories, but because of a growing awareness that there is always yet an-Other perspective to dualistic confrontations. This awareness doesn't seem to be quite captured by a notion like „intercultural competence". I propose instead the notion of „intercultural stance" to express a way of seeing, from the margins so to speak, the relation of Self and Other. The word „stance" is meant to connote precisely this third place and point of view.

Conclusion: The Intercultural Stance

If the communicative era was characterized by the dyad, and the optimistic belief that dyadic interaction and turns-at-talk can solve all problems, the intercultural era decidedly favors the triad or, to borrow a term from the cultural studies scholar Ed Soja in his new book *Thirdspace* (Soja, 1996), the „trialectic" of the individual, the social, and the relational. One could remark that the triadic moment was always inscribed in the Hegelian notion of „dialectic", but after the political demise of Marxism-Leninism, the concept of dialectic seems to have become foreign to many, hence the need to resemiotize it as „trialectic". As the asymmetry of historical memories, but also of power, influence, respectability and wealth, increases within and between our respective societies, it is becoming more appropriate to look not only at the interaction of Self and Other but at the relationality and interdependency of Self and Other. This relationality can only be seen from a third perspective, which Ed Soja calls „critical thirding":

> *„ In this critical thirding, the original binary choice is not dismissed entirely, but is subjected to a creative process of restructuring that draws selectively and strategically from the two opposing categories to open new alternatives. "* (1996:5).

An instance of this critical thirding is precisely the intercultural stance, of which Clifford Geertz writes in *Local Knowledge:*

> *„ To see ourselves as others see us can be eye-opening. To see others as sharing a nature with ourselves is the merest decency. But it is from the far more difficult achievement of seeing ourselves amongst others...a case among cases, a world among world, that the largeness of mind, without which objectivity is self-congratulation and tolerance a sham, comes. "*

(Geertz 1983:16)

References

Anderson, Benedict. 1983. *Imagined Communities*. London: Verso

Anzaldua, Gloria. 1987. *Borderlands/La Frontera: The New Mestiza*. San Francisco: Aunt Lute Book Co.

Bhabha, Homi K. 1994. *The location of culture*. London: Routledge.

Bourdieu, Pierre. 1982. *Ce que parler veut dire*. Paris: Fayard.

Byram, Michael and Geneviève Zarate. 1994. *Définitions, Objectifs ent Evaluation de la compétence socio-culturelle*. Strasbourg: Council of Europe. CC-LANG (94)1.

Geertz, C. 1983. *Local Knowledge*. London: Fontana Press.

Hanks, William. 1996. *Language and Communicative Practices*. Boulder, CO: Westview Press.

Holquist, Michael. 1990, *Dialogism. Bakhtin and his World*. London: Routledge.

LePage, R.B. and Andrée Tabouret-Keller. 1985. *Acts of Identity. Creole-based Approaches to Language and Ethnicity*. Cambridge University Press.

Oller, John W. Jr. 1995. Adding Abstract to Formal and Content Schemata: Results of Recent Work in Peircean Semiotics. *Applied Linguistics* 16:3.

Pratt, Marie Louise. Linguistic Utopias. In N. Fabb, D. Atridge, A. Durant and C. MacCabe. *The Linguistics of Writing*. Manchester: Manchester University Press, 48-66.

Petrilli, Susan. 1993. Dialogism and Interpretation in the Study of Signs. *Semiotica* 97 1/2, 103-118.

Sheriff, John K. 1994. *Charles Peirce's Guess at the riddle. Grounds for Human Significance*. Bloomington, IN: Indiana UP.

Soja, Edward W. 1996. *Thirdspace*. London: Blackwell.

Steele, Ross and Andrew Suozzo. 1994. *Teaching French Culture.Theory and Practice*. Linconlwood, IL: National Textbook Appendices II-V.

van Lier, Leo. 1996. *From Input to Affordance: Social-interactive learning from an ecological perspective*. Unpublished ms.

The Meaning Matrix: A Model for the Study of Intercultural Communication
Øyvind Dahl

One of the difficulties of intercultural communication is that meanings are assigned to words, signs, events or actions by people with different cultural backgrounds. Meanings are not objective and rigid, but the result of life-long negotiation in the process of human interaction. Children learn from their parents and their peers, and gradually they assign certain meanings to certain events, words, and actions. Within a particular social group this means that the members will assign more or less the same meanings to the same events and utterances, thus facilitating a meaningful communication within the group.

When intercultural communication is taking place, the interlocutors may have very different background experiences. They will assign different meanings to the same events and, because this is often done unconsciously, they may feel quite confused when the other person has understood something different from what was intended by the first speaker. For this speaker, in his or her context, the meaning should be quite clear. Nevertheless the communication partner with a different cultural reference frame may have understood something very different.

In this article I shall present a 'meaning matrix', which can be an effective tool for the analysis of such communication problems. The model was developed in my doctoral thesis (Dahl, 1993) in which I studied intercultural communication among the Malagasy (natives of Madagascar) themselves and between Malagasy and Westerners (Europeans) working in rural development projects. In my forthcoming book, (Dahl, 1999), the model is applied to different situations of intercultural communication (communication between members of different nations, age groups, professions, genders, etc). Before the presentation of the model, two different approaches for the study of communication (transmission and semiotics) will be discussed as they will form the basis for the application of the meaning matrix.

The transmission model

The etymological basis of the word communication is the latin word *communis*, which leads to at least two separate significations. One is 'to impart, to transmit'; the other is 'to share' (Oxford, 1982:369). The two different significations have been basic to the development of two different schools in the study of communication, which I label 'the school of transmission' and the 'school of semiotics'.

The school of transmission goes back to the engineers of communication whose main problem was to develop devices able to transmit information from one point to another with the least amount of distortion. The model of two of the pioneers (Shannon and Weaver, 1949) has been reprinted and refined several times.

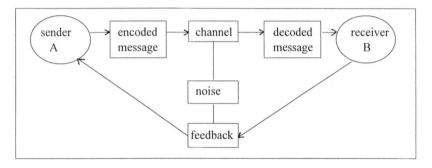

Fig. 1. A model of communication according to the transmission school. (After Shannon and Weaver, 1949)

Essentially the model represents a sender who encodes a message (or a sign) to be transmitted through a channel or medium to the receiver who decodes the message. Noise may cause distortion both to this process of transmission and to the feedback which is the response from the receiver back to the sender.

We shall look at the application of this model when human beings are involved in the process of communication. The model correctly emphasizes that there is a linear aspect in communication; it involves a direct relationship between two communicators, A and B. It is also a causal one. The sender A causes, by means of a signal, certain effects in a receiver B. (For this reason the model has been labeled a 'stimulus – response model' or 'injection model' as A 'injects' an effect at B.) The success of communication can be measured by the extent to which the transmission of the signal (message) can be made with least possible distortion. Within the school of transmission one tries to develop the skills of communication, to formulate precise notions and signs, to reduce sources of noise, to give training for listening in an active way, to give good feedback to the sender in order to enable him or her to make the encoding more precise, thereby facilitating the correct decoding of the signal (message) at the receiver's end.

However, the deficiency of the model lies in the fact that it gives the impression that A can transmit a message to B which – if only the sources of noise can be reduced – will communicate something that is understandable to B. The study of intercultural communication has shown with lots of evidence that this is not always the case. The problem resides in the fact that A and B, who belong to cultures with different experiences or different reference frames, may assign different meanings to the signal (word, sign, event) transmitted. In such cases there is no communication, but miscommunication; there is no mutual agreement about what meaning should be assigned to the signal.

The semiotic model

The semiotic school shifts the focus from the linear aspect of the communication to the sign (greek: *semeion*) which is transmitted. The Swiss linguist Ferdinand de Saussure was concerned with the sign as a physical object with a meaning; or to use his terms, a sign consisted of a 'signifier' and a 'signified'. The signifier is the sign's image as we perceive it – the marks on the paper or the sounds in the air; the signified is the mental concept to which it refers. The relationship between 'signifier' and 'signified' is according to Saussure arbitrary but based on cultural convention broadly common to all members of the same culture who share the same language (1931:158). In Scandianavian languages the 'signifier' and 'signified' are commonly labeled 'uttrykk' and 'innhold' (Martinet, 1976:68), in English, expression and content (Eco, 1976:50). The crucial question is how different people with different cultural backgrounds ascribe meanings (and what meanings) to the signs or signals that are transmitted.

Communication in this semiotic sense does not mean 'sending messages', as is often said. It is a social and mutual 'act of sharing'; it refers to the sharing of concepts, mediated by the use of signs. Communication is, according to this school, about negotiating meanings and how people produce (not merely transmit) meanings. Or, to use a metaphor, human communication is social, about meetings, not mail-boxes. Let us therefore see how people adhere meaning to the signs surrrounding them.

While humans are born into and inhabit a world without meaning, they rapidly invest it with significance and order. As they interact with environments, individual meanings are influenced by 'significant others' (Berger & Luckman, 1966), meanings are negotiated. The social reality is gradually constructed and construed through interaction with other people, with environment, with traditions and thus attains consensus within the group.

The school of semiotics often applies the analogy of a text or a message. The message is a construction of signs which, through interaction with the receivers produce meanings. The sender, defined as transmitter of the message, declines in importance. The emphasis shifts to the text and how it is 'read'. Meaning is created (or produced) when the interpreter (or reader) reads the text (the message) with reference to his or her own stance, experience, and context. The semiotician Umberto Eco contends: "...an expression does not, in principle, designate any object, but on the contrary *conveys a cultural content*" (1976:61). Reading involves negotiation with the text as the reader brings aspects of his or her cultural experience to bear upon the codes or signs which make up the text. Readers with different social experiences or from different cultures may find different meanings in the same text (Fiske, 1990:3).

The sign represents something beyond itself, the referent. The referent is not necessarily a concrete object, it may as well be an abstract or another sign. C. S. Peirce, who is commonly regarded as the founder of the American tradition of semiotics, widened the understanding of the sign when he stated:

> *A sign is something which stands to somebody for something in some respect or capacity. It addresses somebody, that is, creates in the mind of that person an equivalent sign, or perhaps a more developed sign. The sign which it creates I call the* interpretant *of the first sign. The sign stands for something,* its object. (In Fiske, 1990:42)

In Peirce's language 'the interpretant' is not the user of the sign, 'the interpreter', but a mental concept, 'a new sign', produced by the sign and the user's experience of the object. It is an interpretation of the first sign, produced by the help of other signs. The concept of 'interpretant' makes communication into a process which makes it possible to make successive systems of signs interpreting signs, an 'infinite semiosis', in the language of Peirce. Therefore the sign (concrete object or thought) can only be understood as an interaction of the reader in relation to the environment. Without context, there is no text (Hall 1976). The above mentioned concepts can partly be visualized in the figure below.

The relationship between reader, text and referent is essential for the meaning to be produced by the reader. What is meaningful to me as a reader is a matter of what has significance for me: my past experiences, values, feelings and intuitive insights. If the word 'rabbit' is pronounced, it is helpful for the comprehension that I have some experience with this referent. But it is, according to Peirce, not neccessary. For the sign 'rabbit' can also be interpreted by the use of other signs; in fact, this is what we do when we attach meaning to an unknown concept with the help of an encyclopedia which explains a phenomenon or concept by reference to other words or signs. Even when the referent 'witch' is not observed in the concrete world, we can attach meaning to the sign (word or sound).

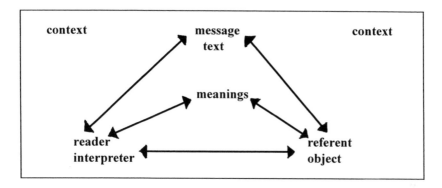

Fig. 2. A semiotic model illustrates how message is created in the field between reader (interpreter), text (message), and referent (object). Adapted from Fiske (1982:4).

Furthermore, it is not only the 'denotation' – the meaning of the word according to some common cultural agreement that counts, but equally well the personal experience I have with a rabbit, the 'connotation'. Does the word evoke good feelings, or disgust, or allergic reactions? The meaning is not hidden in the text or message; it is produced in the encounter with the reader, and his or her former experience. Social background, parents, peers and experienced events through life influence what meaning the reader will assign the message. This assigning of meaning is an ongoing process; it is dynamic. Man is not only a passive receiver, but an active producer of meaning. Meaning is part and parcel of the person. 'Meaning is embodied', say Lakoff and Johnson (1980:196). Meanings are created through human interaction and result from continuous negotiations of meanings.

Since the focus in this aspect is not on transmission, but on the production of meaning, the semiotic school will not say that a communication will experience a breakdown if A and B assign different meanings to a certain event. On the contrary, such behavior must be expected as A and B have different social and cultural backgrounds. Their interpretation is based on different reference frames, different universes of meaning. Different meanings are not necessarily negative. On the contrary, they may represent a source of increased value. The problems of communication may not be due to the process of transmission, but to the different social and cultural universes represented by the individuals in interaction. An improvement of communication can only be obtained when people learn each other's codes of language and cultural background. At least such training may enhance a better understanding of why the other acts and thinks as he or she does.

The meaning matrix

The meaning matrix (Dahl, 1993:31) combines elements from the transmission school and from the semiotic school. It can be seen as a practical tool to be used in the analysis of the communication process when representatives from two different cultures meet. The matrix has a three-part structure beginning with the focus of communication (message), the respective frames of reference of the communicators, and the different meanings that each representative deduces from the other.

The first step will be to define the focus of the communication. The communication may be an exchange of signs, words, (written or spoken), events or other forms of interactions. This 'message' can be interpreted differently from the different cultural standpoints of the interlocutors. The transmission model may help the conceptualization of the process, as sender and receiver generate 'messages' or 'strings of signs'. Furthermore, both coding and decoding, feedback and noise may be involved.

The second step will be to uncover the underlying cultural 'frames of reference' that determine the respective ways of sending and receiving messages. The frames of reference are learned codes which are crucial in a semiotic perspective. The codes are systems into which signs are organized. The frame of reference is concsiously or unconsciously in mind when messages are decoded. One of the problems of communication is that this cultural code is often taken for granted and is out of awareness for the participants of a particular culture. It is the result of a life-long negotiation of meaning and gives rules for the correlation between a signifier and the signified, to use Saussure's language. The goal of this second step of the matrix is to discover specific basic values, norms and attitudes – in short: how meanings are produced respectively within the culture of the communicators. This step necessitates a study of the respective frames of reference (values, norms, priorities, rules, and procedures) that lead to diverging interpretations. The semiotic aspect of the production of meaning will be useful here. General methods developed within the social sciences will apply to discover the frames of references of the two particular cultures involved in the communication.

Finally, the goal of the third step is to deduce the respective meanings that follow from the underlying codes or reference frames of the two partners, and draw conclusions about the communicational encounter that can be analyzed further. The analysis makes possible further studies of the communication process (in the transmission sense) and comparison between the two cultures (in the semiotic sense) as it will uncover different assignments of meanings, sometimes also to identical signs. The procedure will be to delineate what differs in the assignment of meanings (in the semiotic sense), and why communications (in the transmission sense) succeed or break down. Quite often the result is unexpected for the partners, because most often conclusions in a communicational encounter are drawn unconsciously – out of awareness – without deeper reflection.

One case will make clear the procedure. I shall borrow it from my forthcoming book (1999) as an analysis of an encounter between westernized Malagasy students with some tradition-oriented Malagasy farmers.

The case to be described happened in Fihaonana in the outskirts of Antananarivo in Madagascar during the optimistic and promising days following the student's revolt of 1972. One of the slogans of the revolution was "the land to those who cultivate it!" The following account was reported by an informant who was part of a Malagasy student group interacting with the farmers.

A *vazaha* (European) landowner possessed a big plot that he cultivated with the help of paid labour. The *vazaha* had married a Malagasy woman who also worked in the fields. However, the *vazaha* died and the Malagasy woman became old and could not work in the fields any more. So the land was no longer cultivated. Some farmers living in the vicinity of the plot saw all this good, fertile land and wanted to cultivate it. But they did not dare to speak with the old lady and the local authorities.

Some of the students who were involved in the leftist political party, heard about this case. The young idealists were theoretically trained in the doctrines of marxism and socialism and saw a great task in helping the proletarians acquire the land from the big landowner. They organized meetings with the surrounding farmers and were eagerly discussing the procedures to follow. They knew the rules and were willing to go to the authorities to make the necessary steps for the transferring of the land. – The land should belong to those who cultivate it, they argued.

However, a strange thing happened. The students could not get the farmers involved. The farmers said it was a good idea and expressed their gratitude, saying they were going to study the proposal, and they decided to meet again later. But when the students made a new appointment, the farmers postponed the meeting, they talked about all kinds of difficulties and obviously intended to slow down the process. It was impossible to get started. Yet there were no technical problems. The students knew what had to be done, they had the theoretical insight, they knew the necessary procedures to take with the authorities and the law was on their side. But the farmers were not cooperative. They talked about lacking material, wished to wait for a later occasion, and all seemed indifferent.

The contact lasted for several months. Even the enthusiastic students understood that they had to be patient, if progress were to be made. But it seemed illogical that people who expressed their agreement lacked any eagerness in taking action. Especially since every procedure was clear and straight. Finally after having obtained the confidence of the farmers, the reason for the delay was found. Several of the farmers had been employed by the *vazaha* while he was still living. His memory was omnipresent. His old wife was still there, as was his dwelling and agricultural tools. The farmers were afraid of taking his land even even now that he was dead, and even though he had not been a good employer. They feared that he who had become an ancestor *(razana)* and therefore possessed supernatural power, would avenge himself, by causing problems for the living ones. His spirit was surely present in the abandoned fields.

When this explanation was found, a traditional healer *(ombiasy)* was contacted. He prescribed a *'joro'* (sacrifice of an ox accompanied with invocations to the *razana*) at the tomb of the *vazaha* in order to ask him for permission *(miera aminy)*. When this was done, everything was OK, and the land was again cultivated.

The incident can be analyzed by the help of the three steps of the meaning matrix which will be utilized for the schematization of the analysis (see figure 3).

Viewed from outside one can observe that the communication is in crisis because the two partners do not empathize with the world view of the other. Their own reasoning and feelings about the other are based on their own world views.

Both groups agreed on the principle "the land to those who cultivate it", but the different frame of reference or world views caused opposing conclusions and a breakdown of communication since the farmers and the students did not share meanings. The meanings produced, in a semiotic sense, were based on different signs and codes not understood by the two partners of the communication. The students were intrigued by the behaviour of the farmers. At the outset they expressed enthusiasm and gratitude, then reluctancy which developed into indifference and a non-cooperative attitude. The message was

---

1 Focus of the communication

Students: "The land should belong to those who cultivate it."

Farmers: "This is a good principle, which we endorse."

Students: "We must take the necessary steps towards the authorities so that the land can be transferred."

Farmers: "There are some problems, the decision must be postponed."

---

2 Respective cultural 'frames of reference'

STUDENTS – WORLD VIEW:

- The white colonist was a big landowner.
- He has oppressed and exploited the proletarians – the poor farmers.
- This is an example of class struggle.
- We need revolution. The farmers must be made sensitive to the injustice.

FARMERS – WORLD VIEW:

- The land is sacred.
- Fertility depends upon the blessing of the ancestors.
- The spirit of the deceased white man might become angry and retaliate horribly.
- The professional healer must be called upon so that the ancestor's spirits can be invoked properly.

---

3 Meanings deduced from the 'frames of reference'

STUDENTS:

The farmers accept our social analysis, but they do not want to do anything about it.

FARMERS:

The students threaten the harmony. They do not fear the retaliation of the spirits.

Fig 3. Three steps of the meaning matrix.

misinterpreted by the students because they did not have sufficient insight into the world view and the signs of the farmers, even if they all were Malagasy. As explained by the informant:

> *We did not have this religious respect, we did not care about the sacred (hasina), we did not have any personal interest in the land. We did not know the deceased vazaha, and were not afraid of his spirit. We only wanted to help the farmers. We thought we knew the truth. When they said something that resembled what we said, we thought that they had understood. We had to learn to listen with understanding. If a spade had broken in working at the field, they would have interpreted it as a vindicative action by the dead white man.*

We see that in this case it is not important to know whether the referent 'spirit' exist 'objectively' in reality or not. Semiotically speaking, the sign 'spirit' had a cultural content (or represented a 'cultural unit' in the words of Eco (1976:62)). One could say that spirit of the dead man had become an interpretant – a new sign for the farmers.

The farmers' understanding of the students' culture was not any more developed than the students' understanding of the farmers' culture. They had no ideas about marxist class struggle, revolution and exploitation – all meaningful interpretants of marxist thinking for the students.

Many of the technical cadres working in the agricultural programmes in the countryside lack the same cultural insight as these students even when they also are members of the Malagasy culture. The problem of intercultural communication is, as is clearly demonstrated in this case, not only a problem of communication between people from different national cultures such as Norwegian and Malagasy, but a problem of communication, between different world views, and different belief systems concerning the powers of the living and the dead. The correct interpretation of the signs which are utilized in the process demands deeper knowledge of the culture of the other. In this case both groups consisted of Malagasy, but they represented very heterogeneous cultures. Therefore the case also illustrates that problems of intercultural communication are not limited by national borders.

The meaning matrix brings to light how the hidden and unconscious codes or assumptions of a culture may influence the communication between people with different cultural backgrounds. It represents an interpretive approach to the study of intercultural communication. It is not the only one possible, and the choice of factors to be considered is very much up to the investigator and the purpose of the study. However, the meaning matrix is a tool that can be useful for an analysis of episodes that are not immediately clear. In my forthcoming book (1999) several cases from my field studies in Madagascar are presented.

Conclusion

Cultural codes are often hidden and unconscious, sometimes taken for granted by members of a particular culture. However, they are not fixed and unchangeable entities. When people interact and do things together, such codes are constantly established and reestablished and conventions are created as people assign meanings to the texts in their contexts. The semiotic school has illuminated the close connection between culture and the creation of shared meanings by people living together. Through interaction with other people signs are transmitted and interpreted. In such a process meanings are constantly adapted and changed. The meaning matrix has shown that the dynamics of the encoding and decoding processes can be made more comprehensible when they are studied on the basis of the reference frame of each of the participating communicators.

Crucial for the application of the meaning matrix is the exploration of the values, norms and attitudes, in other words, the codes of the cultures. When the underlying cultural assumptions are known, the communication process at the cultural encounter may be more comprehensible. The production of meaning in the semiotic sense can explain the encoding and decoding of meaning in the sense of the transmission school. Thus, the meaning matrix combines the two schools mentioned in the introduction of this article, the semiotic school and the transmission school. Fiske has stated that it is a pity that the proponents of each school have tended to ignore or denigrate the work of the other (1990:190). The introduction of the meaning matrix as a tool for analysis clearly illustrates the usefulness of both schools when they are applied properly.

To conclude, one can say that in intercultural communication total identity of meanings is generally not possible, but an interpretive approach such as demonstrated in the application of the meaning matrix can improve communication. In other words: The more the communicating partners know about the world of meanings (frame of reference) of the Other, and the more they empathize with the Other, the better are the chances for a true and effective communication (Dahl, 1993:190).

The meaning matrix model can be used retroactively to describe a case of communication that has already taken place, or it can be used proactively, to predict possible outcomes or problems in a case of communication to come in the future.

References

Berger, P. L., & Luckmann, T. 1966. *The Social Construction of Reality. A Treatise in the Sociology of Knowledge*. London: Penguin.

Dahl, Ø. 1993. *Malagasy Meanings. An Interpretive Approach to Intercultural Communication in Madagascar*. Stavanger: Misjonshøgskolens Forlag.

Dahl, Ø. 1995. The Use of Stereotypes in Intercultural Communication. In *Essays on Culture and Communication. Language and Cultural Contact. Sprog og kulturmøde No. 10.* Vestergaard, T. (ed.). Center for Languages and Intercultural Studies CSIS, Aalborg: Aalborg University.

Dahl, Ø. 1999. *Meanings in Madagascar. Cases of Intercultural Communication*. Westport, CT: Greenwood Publishing Group.

Eco, U. 1976. *A Theory of Semiotics.* Bloomington: Indiana University Press.

Fiske J. 1990. *Introduction to Communication Studies,* New York: Methuen.

Hall, E. T. 1976. *Beyond Culture.* New York: Doubleday

Lakoff, G., & Johnson, M. 1980. *Metaphores We Live By.* Chicago: Univ. of Chicago Pr.

Martinet, J. 1976. *Hva er semiologi?* Oslo: Gyldendal.

Oxford 1982. *Oxford Latin Dictionary,* Glare, P.G.W. (ed.). Oxford: Clarendon Press.

Saussure, F. de. 1916. *Cours de linguistique générale.* 3ème ed. 1931. Paris: Payot. English version: 1994. Course in general linguistics, Fontana: London.

Shannon, C., & Weaver, W. 1949. *The Mathematical Theory of Communication,* Urbana: Univ. of Illinois Pr.

Intercultural Competence and the Problem of Assessment

Kirsten Jæger

Introduction

According to Byram, Morgan et al. 1994, the question of assessing intercultural competence has not been given much attention by scholars within the field of foreign language teaching (FLT) and cultural studies. However, in order to include intercultural competence as a learning objective in the educational system, reliable and feasible criteria and procedures for assessing intercultural competence have to be developed. The question, I intend to discuss in my paper, is this:

Do the difficulties of establishing evaluation criteria and procedures within the field of cultural learning and acquisition of intercultural competence indicate a more fundamental problem regarding intercultural competence as a learning objective in the educational system? Is it, in fact, difficult to decide whether a person is interculturally competent or not? Is it possible for learners (e.g. university students) to demonstrate intercultural competence in ordinary examination situations?

In my discussion of the topic, I will take as my starting point Chomsky's distinction between the notions competence and performance (Chomsky 1965). Chomsky's concept of competence represents an idealized form of competence which is not realized in normal language usage, and linguists have criticized Chomsky's concept of competence for being unscientific in the sense that the existence of linguistic competence cannot be verified through empirical data, i.e. language usage of native speakers. Unlike Chomsky's idealized competence concept, the concept of *communicative competence,* still influential in the theory and practice of FLT, includes the dimension of communicative practice in the sense that the speaker/hearer proves his/her communicative competence by communicating appropriately with other members of his or her speech community. The question is whether the formulation of the concept of intercultural competence as a learning objective in FLT represents a further development of the concept, a competence concept situated in social interaction or a return to a more idealized and abstract competence concept. In the latter case, it is perhaps not surprising that the problem of assessment, of demonstrating intercultural competent performance in examination situations, has not been debated much among scholars within the field of intercultural competence and FLT.

This is a mainly theoretical paper, although spiced with a number of empirical examples. The empirical examples are taken from teaching and learning reality at Aalborg University, specifically the international study programmes at the university. As a participant in a research project investigating the teaching of intercultural competence at Aalborg University, I (and other researchers involved in the project) have carried out a number of interviews with teachers at the international study programmes at Aalborg University. This study is very limited in scale and is considered to be a pilot study. However, some interesting aspects and tendencies regarding the assessment problem have emerged.

The function of the empirical examples is, of course, to illustrate the theoretical points of view; but also to show the relevance of the assessment problem to the everyday life of teaching and learning at the university and to the general question of how to design international study programmes.

Generally, the points of view presented in this paper aim at higher education and specifically international study programmes. However, the problems can probably be transferred to secondary school level, although testing and assessing qualifications play a more dominating role in tertiary education because of the stronger emphasis on professional/instrumental learning objectives than on general education learning objectives.

The following discussion has two purposes:

1) one purpose concretely related to educational reality, concerning intercultural competence as a didactic and pedagogical aim. That is, a question of more operational kind: can we – as teachers – enhance the development of intercultural competence in our students or pupils; and if this possibility exits, how can we assess that this objective has been attained?

2) another purpose is to contribute to a more concrete and precise discussion of the concept of intercultural competence: if one wants to test if a given learning objective has been reached, one necessarily will have to know what to look for, the criteria to be applied in judging one performance as competent, another as incompetent. Probably one will find the most precise, concrete and well-considered descriptions of the elements and components of intercultural competence in the relatively few texts in the literature where the problems of assessment are addressed.

An inevitable question concerning the assessment problem within foreign language and culture-learning (and probably also in other contexts as well), is the question of the relationship between competence and performance. Can performance be considered to be a direct expression of or even evidence for underlying competence? Or is it possible for the learner to have a higher level of competence than the level he or she at a given moment is able to demonstrate?

In my discussion of the latter topic, I will take as my starting point Chomsky's distinction between competence and performance (Chomsky 1965). Chomsky's concept of competence represents an idealized competence type which is not realized in normal language usage. I shall argue that the concept of intercultural competence is a kind of abstract competence in the sense that it is a competence type which does not necessarily reveal itself in traditional/ordinary examination situations – and consequently a potentially problematic learning objective in the existing educational system.

Empirical Observations

The very limited empirical material from which I draw my examples, consists of interviews with teachers at Aalborg University's international study programmes. The interviews aimed at describing the status quo of teaching intercultural competence at these study programmes: do the teachers see intercultural competence as an important learning objective; does the concept of culture play a major role in their courses; which techniques do they themselves use in order to encourage the acquisition of intercultural competence, etc.

One can distinguish between *three different attitudes* towards the concept of intercultural competence as a learning objective and the possibility of assessing this competence. I do not here consider informants who regard intercultural competence as a totally irrelevant learning objective (in fact, only one informant in a total sample of eleven informants expressed that point of view).

1) Intercultural competence will be developed more or less *automatically*, through the student's participation in an international/intercultural work setting, for example work placement in an international organization (a UN or EU-agency, etc.). The keyword is experience, in the double sense of learning through being involved and participate, being irritated, frustrated, surprised etc. *and* being an experienced person as a result of these learning processes. Acquiring intercultural competence is a question of surviving in a foreign environment. Having survived the period abroad is evidence of the mastery of intercultural competence, no additional evaluation is necessary.

2) Intercultural competence consists of a combination of different elements: knowledge, skills and reflection. An important qualification and part of inter-

cultural competence is an awareness of the complexity of the notion *culture* and awareness of oneself as a culturally influenced individual.

Acquiring intercultural competence is a matter of lifelong learning. As a university teacher, one can provide the students with thinking tools: cultural awareness, an ability to reflect on intercultural experiences, an awareness of influence from one's own cultural background.

The role of the foreign language and/or culture teacher is to *initiate* the process of cultural reflection in the students. The students are themselves responsible for continuing the reflective learning process, when, after having passed the final examinations, they get jobs, which involve participating in international/ intercultural relations. One cannot really assess intercultural competence within the framework of the educational system – for as far as the acquisition of intercultural competence is concerned, the educational process proceeds.

3) Intercultural competence is a necessary learning objective in international study programmes – since the students will be operating in foreign cultures and applying their professional qualifications in foreign culture-environments. As a consequence, intercultural competence should be included in the description of the study programme as *a formal requirement*, and adequate testing procedures will have to be found.

In this study, we operate with one informant group called culture teachers, which means that these teachers teach subjects like Intercultural management, Intercultural communication or Cultural analysis – subjects where the notion of culture is either a core concept or a primary perspective on the topics to be discussed. Interestingly, this (limited and preliminary) pilot study shows that the culture teachers are all in category 2, teachers who find intercultural competence to be very difficult, if not impossible, to assess. We find in category 3 the group of teachers who have the least experience and knowledge concerning cultural learning and the concept of intercultural competence.

However, the point of view expressed by the informants in this category seems reasonable. If intercultural competence is expected to be part of the student's job qualifications, one will have to design appropriate and feasible examination procedures. It is a well-known fact that subjects which are not tested in examination situations, tend to loose importance, seen from the point of view of the students.

State-of-the art in assessing intercultural competence

The state-of-the-art in the Danish educational system is – generally – that intercultural competence is not systematically assessed.

Theoretically, assessment is the aspect of cultural studies and cultural learning which is given least attention. Byram & Morgan et al. mention M. A. Meyer's research (described in Meyer 1991) as a valuable exception from the general tendency to omit the discussion of the assessment problem. His contribution to the discussion of possible assessment methods consists of reporting research results from using mediating exercises in order to assess the student's level of competence. In these exercises – role plays – the student to be assessed plays the role of a mediator between persons from different cultures. Meyer distinguishes between three levels of competence: a monocultural an intercultural and a transculturel level of competence. The highest level of competence (the transcultural level) implies the ability to take into account the cultural background of all participants of the interaction and permit the negotiation and reconsideration of cultural identities, as well.

Byram and Morgan et al. distinguish between three dimensions of intercultural competence: knowledge, attitudes and behaviour; and describe techniques for assessing each dimension:

Knowledge
In relation to the knowledge-dimension, the following aspects can be tested according to Byram and Morgan et al.:
• factual knowledge; explanation of facts from within the foreign culture perspective; description of the appearance and position of the phenomena in contemporary life (e.g. the typical family used in advertising, or the geographical divisions used in weather-forecasting);
• explanation of the significance of the phenomena in shared cultural understandings/meanings;

Attitudes or empathy?
It is potentially dangerous to discuss the assessment of attitudes. One runs the risk of being accused of indoctrination if one wants to test if the students have acquired the (interculturally) correct attitudes.

Byram and Morgan et al. prefer to assess empathy instead – the ability of the student to leave an ethnocentric point of view and identify him/herself with members of the foreign culture. Empathy consists of a cognitively rather than attitudinally oriented dimension.

Behaviour
The behavioural dimension includes an ability to analyze and describe behaviour, and an ability to perform according to norms of the foreign culture as well:

- description and analysis of norms of social interaction in the foreign culture
- performance of social interaction – both verbal and non-verbal – within those norms

The performance of social interaction can be tested in mediation exercises as described by Meyer 1991.

Assessing competence – observing performance

As Michael Byram (Byram 1996) notes – we seek to assess competence but actually – as teachers/evaluators we only have access to performance. But does this situation necessarily constitute a problem?

Let us at first take a look at the traditional examination situation.

Normally, performance in an examination situation is judged as a direct expression of the student's level of competence. For example, in order to test the student's competence in written German, the student is required to write a German essay in four hours without using dictionaries. This is taken to be a direct and reliable method for measuring of the student's proficiency in written German. Of course, one is aware of constraints in the examination situation, the time pressure, the student's anxiety because of the importance of the situation etc. But these factors are not regarded as important enough to consider this examination situation and form to be unreliable as a testing method. For example in marking the essays, the teacher does not take into account that one student has been more nervous than another. He or she only considers the product – the performance – as relevant. External and internal disturbing factors are not considered so important that they are allowed to influence the assessment of the individual student. Performance is considered to be a direct reflection of the underlying competence.

Let us for a moment turn to the person who might be considered to be the founding father of the notions competence and performance and the distinction between them, Noam Chomsky. In the perhaps most frequently cited passage from his *Aspects of a Theory of Syntax* he defines competence as the linguistic knowledge of

> *"an ideal speaker-listener in a completely homogeneous speech-community who knows its language perfectly and is unaffected by such grammatically irrelevant conditions as memory limitations, distractions, shifts of attention and interest, and errors (random or characteristic) in applying his knowledge of the language in actual performance."*
> (Chomsky 1965:3)

Clearly, according to Chomsky, competence does not reveal itself fully in our normal faulty performance. Performance is influenced by psychological constraints, lack of concentration on the part of the speaker, and different disturbing factors in the environment. Consequently, performance is normally not perfect, in the sense of meeting the standards of grammatical correctness. However, competence exits, in the speaker/hearer's intuition of grammatical correctness, his or her ability to judge whether the performance of others meets the standards of grammaticality. The reason why competence can be perfect, is that linguistic competence is considered to be an innate competence. One cannot explain the development of linguistic competence in children as a process of merely processing the linguistic data they meet in their environment. Thus Chomskyan linguistic competence is not directly reflected in linguistic performance.

The Chomskyan focus on the *idealized* speaker/hearer in the homogeneous speech community has given rise to strong criticism from a sociolinguistic perspective. Hymes (1972) ironically compares the Chomskyan idealism with a Garden of Eden-view – competence representing the state before the linguistic fall, represented by the performance. According to Hymes, speech communities are *not* homogeneous in the first place – and the idealized speaker/hearer is likely to be institutionalized (still according to Hymes) because such a creature would be lacking the must fundamental abilities of acceptable communicative behaviour. In other words, Chomsky's ideal of a speaker/hearer lacks *communicative* competence – the competence to make one's communicative contribution an appropriate one in normal, real-life social interaction.

How does Hymes see the relationship between performance and *communicative* competence? Is it possible to be communicatively competent and communicate in a way that is unacceptable and inappropriate to other members of the speaker/hearer s speech community. Clearly, this is not the case, due to the fact that appropriateness is *included* in the *definition* of communicative competence. Meeting the standards of communicative acceptability in one's performance is demonstrating communicative competence. And other members of one's speech community possess the authority to decide whether or not the performance is competent.

Probably, Hymes in his critique of Chomsky makes a first contribution to questioning the competence-performance-distinction. His contribution re-presents an attempt to integrate the aspect of „making it work" in practice into the concept of linguistic competence. But the integration of successful practice as a criterion for competence leads to a gradually increasing relativization of the ideal requirements to linguistic correctness and pragmatic appropriateness. In accordance with a more practice orientered competence concept, Kasper describes the communicative competence concept of modern communication theory as simply the ability to communicate successfully or, at least, successfully to the extent that major communication problems and misunderstandings do not occur during conversation.

> *[Es ist]* "nützlich daran zu erinnern, daß kommunikative Kompetenz in der Kommunikationswissenschaft nicht als die Idealnorm postuliert wird, als die Hymes und Habermas sie konzeptualisiert haben. Vielmehr wird kommunikative Kompetenz als die Fähigkeit angesehen, Probleme zu vermeiden und Interaktionen und Beziehungen so zu handhaben, daß es geht oder gut genug ist." (Kasper 1996: 38)

Intercultural competence revisited

Earlier we observed that, in the educational system, performance traditionally and normally is viewed as a direct reflection of underlying competence. But how is the relationship between competence and performance conceptualized in the discussion of *intercultural competence?*

Considering the early research in intercultural competence, it aimed at preparing (primarily) American business people to operate in foreign cultures. The evidence of the individual's mastery of intercultural competence was his / her degree of economic or commercial success. Successful performance was seen as an indication of competence. However, other factors may contribute to success or failure, the complexity of the task, the degree of foreign-ness of the other culture – a person with a given level of intercultural competence can be successful in some settings, but not in others. As intercultural competence is discussed as a learning objective in the educational system, the need to find and discuss appropriate assessment procedures becomes evident.

The formulation of intercultural competence as a new learning objective in foreign language learning emphasizes that the linguistic and cultural competence of the foreign language learner should not be measured against native speaker criteria and norms, expressed as the standard of *communicative competence.* The transfer of the communicative competence-concept from the area of native speakers to the area of foreign language learners is fundamentally wrong.

Thus Byram in 1996:

> "Nonetheless, in adopting these new perspectives (Hymes, Halliday), foreign language teachers perpetuated an error which has been inherent in the traditions of the last hundred years. This was the adoption of a descriptive model of native speaker competence in interaction with other

native speakers, as a basis for teaching a foreign language. For many years this led to language learners being expected to aim at native speaker ability in mastering the grammar of a language. When performance was judged almost exclusively in terms of reading and writing, some learners managed to approach this standard. The shift in emphasis to performance in the spoken language – with the pressures and constraints of real-time production – made it clear that the native-speaker model is an impossible target, and therefore condemns all learners and their teachers to failure. ...Although Hymes, Halliday and others were concerned with describing native speakers, their models were adopted without question or modification by foreign language teachers and theorists (Byram 1996: 59)

The refusal to apply native speaker criteria and norms in assessing language learners creates a problem, though. Because: which standards are we to apply, if we cannot apply the standards of the foreign language and culture? *The intercultural speaker* – Byram's model of the language learner exits in a sort of vacuum where he/she is assessed according to his /her ability to act as a mediator between cultures.

Clearly, there is a need to discuss how one should discuss the intercultural speaker-standards in a more explicit and concrete way: are they equally relevant to all pupils/students who are supposed to acquire intercultural competence? Is it relevant to apply the mediator-exercise everywhere, where intercultural competence should be assessed?

To Byram and Morgan et al. it is clearly not the case that performance automatically reflects competence, or that competence can simply be understood as the ability to perform well at a given time, for example an examination situation. Competence may be on a higher level than what is actually demonstrated in performance. In relation to the mediating-exercises, Byram and Morgan et al. suggest the use of introspection and reflection on one's performance as part of the overall examination procedure. Thus, students' ability to reflect on and to explain their own behaviour is considered part of their intercultural competence. This indicates, too, that intercultural competence is more than the ability to perform successfully: if performance is considered to be a direct reflection of competence, the motivations leading to competent behaviour are irrelevant.

Byram and Morgan et al. demonstrate a truly Chomskyan way of conceptualizing the relationship between competence and performance in discussing the fact that a student may demonstrate different levels of competence during one examination performance. What mark should be given for this performance?

Traditionally, the teacher would estimate the mean value of the performance –
but:

> *"This may be defensible as a means of establishing an examination*
> *evaluation but it masks the fact that, if the constraints of a particular*
> *moment are reduced and sufficient conditions created, then a more direct*
> *exhibition of underlying competence can be achieved. And it is this*
> *underlying competence that examinations purport implicitly to measure"*
> (Byram & Morgan et al.: 173)

Concluding remarks

A comparison between the different concepts of competence shows that the
notion of intercultural competence represents a move towards a more abstract
and mentalistic view of competence. Students may be interculturally competent,
but due to unfavourable constraints demonstrate lower levels of competence.
This means that there is no direct and unproblematic relationship between competence and performance. The student may demonstrate intercultural competence
in an examination situation but one cannot be sure that the student will in fact
demonstrate the level of competence he or she actually masters. Even examination techniques specifically designed for assessing intercultural competence,
as the mediator exercises (Meyer 1991) cannot be regarded as fully reliable
measurement methods in relation to the student's level of competence.

The assumption that the relationship between competence and performance
is an indirect and potentially problematic one, is probably one reason why the
assessment problem has been more or less ignored in intercultural competence
research. Another reason may be the inherent attitudinal dimension of intercultural competence which on the one hand is judged important but one the other
hand is difficult to assess because of the ethical aspect (assessing attitudes might
be considered to be a kind of indoctrination).

In recent publications, Michael Byram adds a fourth dimension to the overall
concept of intercultural communication: a dimension called savoir-apprendre
(Byram 1995). Savoir-apprendre can be described as a learning ability: the overall ability to reflect upon and learn from one's experiences; almost an academic
qualification. This dimension is not discussed in relation to the assessment problem by Byram and Morgan et al. However, a consideration of the savoir-
apprendre dimension might be a productive point of departure for a discussion
of assessment. A number of informants (teachers) from the pilot study suggest
that the student's work placement abroad or university studies abroad should be

used as an occasion for assessing intercultural competence in practice. It is also quite evident that the students apply very different learning strategies during their stay abroad. Some students regard their stay abroad as a kind of special offer, arranged by their home university; an offer which either does or does not live up to their expectations. In the latter case, the learning profit for the student is rather limited. Other students actively fight circumstances which impede their learning opportunities and seek actively to bring themselves in situations where they can strengthen their knowledge and skills in relation to the foreign country's language and culture, for example through participation in leisure activities, sport, jobs in their spare time (in cases of university study); for example, one student took a job as a waitress because she felt the need to practice her oral proficiency in German, and because she wanted to experience other parts of German culture than university life.

In other words: obviously one can observe different levels of savoir-apprendre in a given group of students. This indicates that it would be worth-while to explore work-placement and university studies abroad as opportunities not only for acquiring, but also for assessing intercultural competence.

References

Byram, M., Morgan, C., and Colleages. 1994. *Teaching-and-Learning Language-and-Culture* Clevedon: Multilingual Matters.

Byram M. 1995. Acquiring Intercultural Competence. A Review of Learning Theories. *Intercultural Competence. A New Challenge for Language Teachers and Trainers in Europe* Sercu, L. Aalborg: Aalborg University Press.

Byram, M. 1996. Cultural Learning and Mobility: The educational challenge for foreign language teaching. *Interkulturelle Dimensionen der Fremdsprachenkompetenz* Ambos, E. Bochum: AKS-Verlag.

Chomsky, N. 1965. *Aspects of a Theory of Syntax*, Cambridge, Massachusetts,

Hymes, D., 1972. On Communicative Competence. *Sociolinguistics* Pride, J.B. & Holmes, J. Harmondsworth: Penguin.

Kasper, G. 1996 Wessen Pragmatik? Für eine Neubestimmung fremdsprachlicher Handlungskompetenz. *Interkulturelle Dimensionen der Fremdsprachenkompetenz* Ambos, E. Bochum: AKS-Verlag.

Meyer, M. 1991. Developing transcultural competence. Case studies of advanced foreign language learners. *Mediating Languages and Cultures. Towards an Intercultural Theory of Foreign Language Education* Byram, M., Buttjes, D. Clevedon: Multilingual Matters.

Language and Culture: Disconnection and Reconnection

Karen Risager

The phrase "language and culture are intimately connected" is often heard among people who are engaged in language teaching and learning and studies of inter-cultural communication. The phrase may be put stronger: "language and culture are inseparable". This general claim lays behind the development of research areas such as cultural studies within language teaching and learning (Byram and Morgan 1994, Kramsch 1993, et al.). The connection between language and culture is often stated as a truism, and rests on a solid tradition dating back into the 18th and 19th centuries, where a number of philosophers and writers developed the national romantic idea of an intimate relationship between lan-guage, culture, people and nation.[1] Other phrases that seem to presuppose an unproblematic relationship between language and culture are: "language and its culture" and "language is culture, and culture is language".

The fundamental point of view in this article[2] is that it is necessary to start from processes of globalization caracterizing the world today. They affect the linguistic domain: languages spread all over the world as a consequence of e.g. migration and international technologies of communication and information, most of all English.[3] And they affect the cultural and societal domain in the broad sense in the form of worldwide homogenizing and heterogenizing tenden-cies (Robertson 1995, Wilson and Dissanayake 1996). The linguistic, cultural and social complexity arising from these developments makes the claim of an exclusive relationship between language and culture more unjustified than ever.

In what follows, I will introduce a distinction between three different concep-tions of culture in relation to language (Part I), then I will discuss each of these conceptions from a theoretical point of view, including the concepts of discon-nection and reconnection (Part II), and in the end I will discuss how language teaching copes or may cope with recent developments related to this issue (Part III).

Part I: Three conceptions of culture in relation to language

Discourse associated with the fields that are especially interested in language and culture (the teaching of culture as part of language teaching, intercultural

communication) seems to merge three different conceptions of culture in relation to language, or three different perspectives on the relation language-culture:

a. Culture as contained in the pragmatics and semantics of language (Ca)[4]

b. Culture as macro-context for language use (Cb)

c. Culture as thematic content in the discourse of language teaching (Cc)[5]

In both a, b, and c one can point out cases in which language and culture may be
disconnected:

* First we see an increasing acceptance of non-native, but still well-functioning
  linguistic competence, i.e. a competence whose pragmatic and semantic (as
  well as grammatical and phonological) components comprize more than they
  do when the language is used as a native language. These components are
  influenced by e.g. the speaker's first language.

* Secondly we see an increase in the tendency of recontextualization of languages, as both 'big' and 'small' languages are constantly being transplanted
  to new environments as a result of migration and communication by international media.

* Thirdly we see in the context of teaching an increasing tendency of dissociation of language and content as opposed to traditional language teaching, in
  the sense that topics in language teaching do not need to concentrate on the
  culture of the target country/ies.

Besides these three conceptions of culture and language I want to point out a
conception that belongs to the generic level, i.e. it relates to the concepts of
'language as such' and 'culture as such', illustrated by a statement such as:
'there is no culture without language, and there is no language without culture'.
This general anthropological/philosophical claim, which I subscribe to, can also
be found in the discourse on language and culture, but I shall not give it further
comments here. The three conceptions (or perspectives) that I will discuss, all
belong to the differential level, as they relate to specific languages and specific
cultures. They also represent three different ways in which linguistics and
sociolinguistics approach the cultural field.

   My own frame of reference for the discussion of culture and society may be
found:

* in the anthropological thinking about cultural complexity (Barth 1991,
  Hannerz 1992): the idea that any society is compozed of a number of discourse

communities characterized by certain meanings and interpretations, partly expressed in the uses of language, and

- in the sociological thinking about globalization (Robertson 1995, Wilson and Dissanayake 1996): the idea that the world today experiences an intensified dual process of homogenization and heterogenization, creating two focalizations at the same time: the global and the local.

Part II: Theoretical discussion

Culture as contained in the pragmatics and semantics of language (Ca)

Any natural language develops as part of the social practice of a community of language users. These communites may be of different sizes, from e.g. a family to an international network of researchers within a certain field. They are built up around a social structure and will to a greater or lesser extent be characterized by a common frame of reference and common norms and values. The social structure, as well as frames of reference, norms and values, leave their marks on language in its pragmatics and semantics. As examples one might mention culturally specific genre conventions and rhetorical norms, politeness norms, and, especially in the domain of lexis: the use of metaphors in different cultures, as well as the cultural history of important parts of the vocabulary, as it has been studied by e.g. R. Williams 1976 (1988).

Thus language organizes and expresses a whole range of cultural information and interpretations of concepts and ways of life that have got their specific form as part of the development of the specific community of language users. In this sense language contains culture, it carries its culture within it. We are talking here about language structure (or with Halliday 1978: the 'meaning potential' of the language), and the relationship between the language structure and the culture within which it has developed, has been discussed ever since Sapir and Whorf expressed their views on the determining influence of the language structure on thought and cognition, referred to by Fishman 1971 as 'the language constraint view', as opposed to 'the language reflection view' which states that the language structure only reflects the culture in question.

However, it is necessary to specify that this only applies to language outside acquisition contexts. The person who is acquiring a new language, typically uses this language without any awareness of the cultural dimension of language, especially in the initial phases. It cannot be avoided that the new language is at first conceived mostly as a code whose pragmatics and semantics have to be supplied by the learner himself/herself, among other things on the basis of his/her own mother tongue. The acceptance of this interlanguage as a specific type of language (cf. e.g. Faerch, Haastrup and Phillipson 1984) means acceptance of the existence of types or varieties of a language that do not have an exclusive relationship to the cultural community in which the language has developed. I will come back to this later on.

What concept of culture is associated with Ca?

Ca presupposes a relatively narrow concept of culture, in so far as only the parts of the whole that have been linguistically coded are referred to. It is a conception of culture that assigns a decisive role to linguistic communication, as well as concepts and conceptual networks. One might say that this conception of culture orients itself towards the interface with language. It is hardly a coherent concept of culture, as the cultural elements referred to do not have any internal systematic structure nor dynamics other than the linguistic.

   This conception represents the more traditional way in which linguistics approaches the cultural field, especially as regards lexis. There is a long tradition of interest in the cultural history of the vocabulary, the spread of loan-words, etc.

Culture as macro-context for language use (Cb)

Language typically develops and is codified in a broader social and societal context. Anyone working within pragmatics and the sociology of language would maintain that language use must be seen in its relationship with the social and societal context in which it functions, cf. e.g. Fairclough 1992 who emphasizes the dialectical relationship between language use (discourse) and social structure: 'Discourses do not just reflect or represent social entities and relations, they construct or 'constitute' them . .' (p. 3). This view has been partly anticipated by Fishman 1971, who writes: 'language behavior feeds back upon the social reality that it reflects and helps to reinforce it (or change it) in accord with the values and goals of particular interlocutors' (p. 352).

   What Fishman 1971 (or Fairclough 1992) do not do, is to distinguish between contexts where the language is used as a first language, and contexts where the language is used as a foreign or second language, i.e. native and non-native contexts. This distinction, however, is necessary in fields such as the study of intercultural communication and language teaching and learning. One of Fishman's basic concepts may be used to describe this distinction, namely congruence: Fishman says that language use may be congruent with certain social domains and incongruent with certain others. Similarly we may say that a language used as a foreign language in the learner's own country is used in an incongruent macro-context.

In the native context there has been a continuous development over a long historical period, so that one can speak of a dialectical co-development of language and culture. Social and cultural practice has contributed to the development of linguistic practice and vice versa, and political and hegemonic relations of dominance have favoured some linguistic and cultural variants to the detriment of others.

In this connection I am especially thinking of macro-contexts of the size of the nation state, such as Britain, Denmark etc., because the frame of reference of the argument is foreign language acquisition, learning and teaching, which normally aims at the nationally codified norm of the language, especially in the case of linguistic production. But contexts may in theory be of many types, depending upon categories of linguistic variation. E.g. the Danish island of Funen is the native context for Funen dialects, and the Danish educational system is the native context for a number of didactic registers of Danish language. The (macro)-context may be big in size, e.g. the global production and distribution structure, or small, e.g. a small firm.

Recontextualization of languages

A non-native context, then, is a context where a 'foreign' language has been introduced, and is used for a short period of time or more permanently: the language has been recontextualized. It may be just a casual event, such as e.g. Finnish speaking tourists visiting Denmark, but otherwise it is the more permanent cases that are the most interesting, e.g. the slow increase in the use of English in Denmark, which may result in a certain degree of integration (Preisler 1998), also described as a development in the direction of second language status. Or the use of other foreign languages in more restricted contexts within the education system, in internationally oriented business and organizations, in imported films, books, etc. Likewise the introduction of the various minority languages in Denmark, with the forms of linguistic integration that this development results in, e.g. codeswitching. Recontextualization has a starting point which is naturally discontinuous, but as the language in question begins to interact with the new cultural context, a continuous development is created, resulting in a greater or lesser degree of 'nativization' (Kachru 1986, Berns 1990). Thus language and culture are reconnected in a new relationship.

Until now I have been discussing macro-contexts: societal, geographical etc. structures that regulate social, cultural and linguistic life. But what about micro-contexts and what happens to them in the course of recontextualization? By a micro-context I mean the immediate situational context of linguistic communication or interaction. It is important to notice that this micro-context is partly created by the interaction process itself. E.g., institutionally given roles and norms may be affirmed, denied or changed by virtue of expectations and interpretations actualized in the interaction process.

When a language is recontextualized, parts of the micro-context may accompany it in the form of culturally specific potentials for action and interpretation related to norms and values that are characteristic of the native context. When native speakers of French, for example, travel to Denmark, the micro-context goes with them in the shape of their dispositions to use the language in accordance with cultural practice in their home country. When the language is introduced by way of a film, the content of the film, e.g. scenes in the narrative sequence, may represent visual and auditory dimensions of the native micro-context. When some language is spoken as a foreign language by a Dane, it may be the case that his or her language use is totally devoid of any aspects of the native micro-context: no native frames of reference, no reference to native norms and values. On the other hand, there may be cases where comprehensive systems of potential micro-contexts accompany recontextualization, as e.g. when half a village moves from one country to another, bringing along a varied cultural space.

With the growing globalization – migration, tourism, cultural export etc. – we see more and more often that languages are recontextualized, both 'big' languages with a large international diffusion, such as English and French, and 'small' languages, which are chiefly spread through migration. The linguistic[6] and cultural complexity (Hannerz 1992) that is a consequence of this process, results in a number of incongruences that create some difficulties for the fields of language teaching and intercultural communication. These disciplines have to cope with the fact that language and culture are disconnected and reconnected in new ways. I shall return to the pedagogical aspects of this state of affairs later on.

What concept of culture is associated with Cb?

In the conception of culture as native or non-native macro-context for a language, we have a quite broad concept of culture like the one we find within anthropology, especially within ethnography, as it has to do with localized, contemporary social structures, ways of life, norms, values and beliefs, of a kind that ethnographers would investigate during field work. It is a concept of culture that covers both forms of practice, forms of thought and cognition, the societal and social structure, and the natural (geographical) basis, so it is a quite comprehensive concept. Still, it is restricted to being a *context*, and it is restricted to the *here-and-now*, being regarded as a context for contemporary uses of language in their potential (localized) micro-contexts.

This conception of culture represents the way modern sociolinguistics usually approaches the cultural field, even if sociolinguists as a rule prefer using concepts like social structure, social system, etc., because the word culture has been reserved for neighbouring disciplines: Anthopology studying the cultural dimension of social life: values, belief systems etc.; and studies of literature and art, which focus on culture in yet another sense.

Halliday is one of the sociolinguists who has stressed the importance of the social dimension of language use (Halliday 1978, Halliday and Hasan 1989), and Fairclough, who as far as linguistics is concerned, builds upon Halliday's 'systemic grammar', has succeeded in working out a consistent integration of parts of sociological theory with the linguistic analysis of texts in what he calls the three dimensions of discourse analysis: 1. the linguistically orientated analysis of the text (oral or written) as a product, 2. the analysis of discursive practice: the production, distribution and reception of the text, and 3. the analysis of social practice: the role of the text/the discursive practice in the constitution of the societal practice on the basis of the specific position of the text in the power structure and the hegemonic structure (e.g. Fairclough 1992).

Natural languages do not become culturally neutral by recontextualization

It is useful to distinguish, with Halliday 1978, between the 'meaning potential' of a language, and the 'actual linguistic choice'. When a language is recontextualized, its meaning potential goes with it, but may be extended with more or less isomorphic meaning potentials deriving from the new macro-context. Thus a spread of the language to new contexts results in an extension of its meaning potential. It does not become culturally neutral, rather one might say that it becomes an instance of cultural syncretism.

When a language is used as a foreign language, its meaning potential is taken over, but the learners still do not have sufficient knowledge of it, and have to supplement it with meaning potential from their own mother tongue and perhaps other sources ('interference'). Thus, even in its early phases, the interlanguage of the learners is not culturally neutral, but contains meaning potential from both languages involved (and perhaps others). Gradually the learners acquire a better understanding of the native meaning potential and may use it, but they are still able to use their 'original' meaning potential in communication with other people from their own country. I here refer to the meaning of the concept 'interlanguage' as it is developed in Faerch, Haastrup and Phillipson 1984, p. 272: 'an interlanguage is a variety of language which exists in a contact situation between a learner's L1 and L2. According to this, an interlanguage typically has features in common with both a learner's L1 and with the L2'.

Whereas some people seem to think that e.g. English is culturally neutral in lingua franca communication, I would say that this is completely wrong. It has in fact an enlarged meaning potential coming from two or more macro-contexts. In that way there is greater elasticity in lingua franca communication, but also potentially less precision. Even if there exists an enlarged meaning potential, the actual linguistic choice may be more restricted, as interlocutors will orient themselves towards each other in the communication situation in question ('negotiate'), and end up with some ad hoc compromise influenced by power relations and the interlocutors' levels of linguistic and communicative competence. Perhaps it is typically the intersection of the different meaning potentials that is used (if there is an intersection!), so that for example fewer politeness forms are used, and words are used with a meaning strongly marked by the immediate situation.

Culture as thematic content in the discourse of language teaching (Cc)

In principle a language may express any thematic content – if this can at all be verbalized. There is no necessary connection between the language one uses and the topic one talks or writes about.[7] But there may be said to exist some congruence phenomena, in the sense that the conceptual structure of the language may be more apt to express entities and relations rooted in the native context than other languages are. Cf. the following passage from Schlesinger 1991, p. 22: 'It is widely held that, in principle, everything that can be said in one natural language, can be said in every other one', but: '. . there are differences in the ease with which a given distinction can be made in various languages'.

What concept of culture is associated with Cc?

This question presupposes that there is a concept of culture here, but I think that in fact there is none. One cannot speak of a concept of culture in this situation, as any verbalizable content is possible, from ablatives to zombies.

The conception of culture that exists in practice in language teaching – and here we have in fact a concept of culture – has been defined exclusively on political and educational grounds, and I will come back to that later. Traditionally, linguistics is not concerned with the thematic content of texts. Linguistics – discourse analysis, conversational analysis – is chiefly interested in how pragmatic relations and discursive structures influence and develop the message, but is as a rule not interested in the message itself, and how it may contribute to our knowledge of the world and of ourselves. Maybe this state of affairs is changing. Fairclough is at any rate an example of a theorist who adresses himself both to linguistic and ethnomethodological fields of study, and to sociology and history (Foucault, Gramschi et al.).

Part III: Pedagogical discussion

Culture as contained in the pragmatics and semantics of language (Ca)

In language teaching there is a strong demand that the teaching develop learners' awareness that the rules for use and the meaning system of the foreign or second language often are not identical with those of their first language, and that the interlanguage of the learners has to aim at – but not necessarily attain – the native language with its specific pragmatics and semantics. In this connection I define the native language as those pragmatic and regional variants of the standard form of the target language that it is suitable and realistic to aim at in the teaching. Another question is of course how one defines the standard form of the target language, as one has to choose between regional variants each with its official status, e.g. British English, American English, etc.

The attempt to get learners' interlanguage to become as native-like as possible is seen as an important part of the teaching of linguistic awareness, and consists typically in pointing out pragmatic and semantic differences between the foreign language and the learners' own language, thereby showing that some linguistic phenomena are culturally specific. These comments are of a contrastive nature, probably often asymmetric, in the sense that the teaching focuses on the cultural dimension of the foreign language and not on that of the first language. Typically these commentaries will have an ad hoc character, as they are introduced at moments where learners need some information in order that their understanding and production of any particular text may be as native-like as possible.

This teaching of linguistic awareness is also a teaching of cultural awareness, but only in the restricted sense I discussed above, since only the parts of the whole that have been linguistically coded are referred to.

As long as the only aim of (the linguistic side of) language teaching is native language use, one can maintain an intimate relationship between language and culture (in the sense of Ca: culture as contained in the language). But in some respects the idea of the native speaker model is being questioned. First, it must be accepted that as a rule it is an illusion to believe that the learner can attain complete native linguistic competence. That means an acceptance of the so-called 'near-native speaker', who has a linguistic (including a pragmatic and a semantic) competence which is not quite identical with that of a native speaker (we leave out of account the problem of defining the native standard language user!). Secondly some people react to the expression 'near-native speaker' because it gives the impression of an insufficient 'native speaker'. Therefore another expression has been coined: 'the competent speaker'. Thirdly some people (Byram and Zarate 1994) point to the fact that the non-native speaker has some possibilities of mediation between languages and between cultures that may justify the use of still another expression: 'the intercultural speaker', i.e. a person who is capable of perceiving and explaining cultural and linguistic differences, and of making use of this capability in communication. In these situations, the preferred aim within the frames of language teaching is probably still native language use, but this may be supplemented and balanced by other types of norms, so that one uses other evaluation criteria as well in dealing with linguistic competence.

Furthermore, studies of language acquisition and learning have created an interest in learners' interlanguage as a language in its own right with its own potential for communication. This means a certain acceptance of the inter-language, even at early stages, as being 'good enough' to be used in commu-nication with foreigners, and learners are encouraged to use their interlanguage outside the classroom, including in situations where the target language to be used as a lingua franca. There are good pedagogical reasons for often using the target language in lingua franca situations, partly in order to get learners to know more about the areas and domains of distribution of the language, partly to strengthen learners' communicative self-confidence (Risager 1996a).

So, to the extent that one abandons the native speaker as the only model of language teaching, one loosens the exclusive relationship between the target language and the culture that it contains in its pragmatics and semantics.

Culture as macro-context for language use (Cb)

In language teaching there is a strong tradition of preferring to work, as much as possible, with the target language in its native context. Teaching materials typically show communication going on in countries where the language is spoken as a first language, so that learners can get an impression of the wider context for the use of that particular language. Materials deriving from target language countries are extensively used, and native guest teachers are invited into the classroom in order to demonstrate native language use by a person who carries with him or her the micro-context in his or her dispositions for the use of the language. Study visits and exchanges typically go to target countries.

What is especially focused on in the native context, is the everyday knowledge and capabilities that one has to have in order to be able to participate in social life at least as a visitor, e.g. as a tourist on a short visit. It is concrete factual know-ledge of elementary geography, transport and everyday consumption: where are the towns, how can one travel in the country, where can one buy what, what is the climate like? It is a practically orientated, phenomenological understanding of culture, one might call it 'a thin description', following the semiotic anthropologist Geertz (1973).

But some people also want to go more into depth with the insight into the foreign country, maybe in a more hermeneutical direction, asking questions like: What happens in interaction between people in diffferent situations and different milieus? How do they perceive the situation, and how do we perceive it? What does it mean to people to live in this country or this locality? What identities do they have? This is called 'thick description' by Geertz (1973), who says about this: 'the whole point of a semiotic approach to culture is . . to aid us in gaining access to the conceptual world in which our subjects live so we can, in some extended sense of the term, converse with them'. (p. 24).

As mentioned above, study and exchange visits chiefly go to target language countries, and for this purpose ethnographically inspired methods are developed in order to study the here-and-now context for language use in the locality to which the journey goes. By the way, when learners go to the target language country, they often meet a number of incongruences in the sense that the standard language they have learnt, in many cases does not correspond to the local context. Some places people may speak another sociolect, or they may speak the target language as second language in an ethnic minority context. As it becomes more and more usual in the teaching to get personal experience with interaction with native speakers, whether it be through travels or through guest teachers and students, the attitude towards linguistic variation will probably become more open than is normally the case today, not only with respect to linguistic reception, but also with respect to linguistic production.

However, the principle of going to the target language country/ies and study the native context in some locality is no longer absolute. Even if the majority of exchange visits from e.g. Denmark go to countries where the target language is spoken as a first language, quite a few study visits of other kinds go to other countries where the language functions as a foreign language, e.g. English in Finland, Poland, Latvia, Germany, or German in The Czech Republic. In those cases learners get into contact with non-native macro-contexts that they will have to cope with, contexts that are incongruent with the language they communicate in. There are also many learners who correspond with other people than native speakers through e-mail networks combining schools in different countries. There are good reasons for using these kinds of contact once in a while in order to demonstrate the possibilities of broad human contact by way of the target language.

Culture as thematic content in the discourse of language teaching (Cc)

General language teaching and learning has for many years had a double objective: to learn the language and to gain in insight into the culture and the society of the country/ies where the language is spoken. Topics relating to just these countries have been preferred (focusing on the central countries: Britain/ USA, Germany, France etc.), and topics that are cross-cultural in character or relate to other discplines (biology, technology, etc.) have received lower priority. Teaching materials typically deal with the ways of life, literature, history, and social structure of the (large) target language countries, often justified by general educational principles of insight into the national history and culture of the country.

This is an even broader conception of culture than the anthropological one discussed above. Beside contemporary society and culture it includes the historical dimension, thus the study of the history of literature and of culture in general has its place here. It also focuses more on work with fiction, which represents alternative worlds in the past, present, and future. It is an almost encyclopedic conception of culture and society, but still not all-embracing or universal: it is still conceived within the borders of the nation state and its development.

However, this national orientation of the content of language teaching - which dates back to the 19th century – is declining. One may say that the national epoch of language teaching is coming to an end (cf. Risager 1997). In these years we see a development towards a greater and greater dissociation between language and culture in contrast to the traditional connection that has just been described.

An important tendency is that foreign language teaching and to a lesser degree second language teaching is moving in an intercultural direction. There is a growing awareness that through studies of cultures in the foreign countries learners may become more aware of their own cultures, and that it may be a good idea that learners read texts and produce texts themselves in the foreign language about their own country or locality. In such a case the traditional connection between language and culture has been broken, and a new kind of connection is shaped. However, we are still within the national paradigm, as it is typically two national cultures that are implicitly or explicitly compared.

Another tendency is the above-mentioned pattern of international exchanges in these years where learners travel to non-target language countries. In these cases the topics studied by the learners may have nothing to do with culture and society in target language countries. Teachers and learners have to cope with life and conditions in other localities.

A similar tendency is the pattern of international e-mail correspondence. Learners of English in Denmark who correspond with learners of English in Netherland, Greece, France, Germany etc. may of course gather about a topic that is related to Britain, but they need not do that. Learners may use their time to tell each other about their own cultures, or something quite different.

In classroom teaching we also see some tendencies to loosen the connection to target countries, as cross-cultural topics or general topis such as human rights and environmental issues are becoming more popular. One might also mention the increase in the use of translations of literature from other countries.

Last, but not least, one should mention the development toward using the foreign language as language of instruction for other disciplines, partly in shorter periods of cross-disciplinary collaboration, partly in whole programmes accomplished in one or more foreign languages. For immigrants and refugees this is the normal situation, as they are taught all disciplines in their second language (except foreign languages).

Thus there are many instances of dissociation between language and culture at the Cc level. This situation may be welcomed, as it allows foreign language teaching to demonstrate the general usefulness of the target language as far as topic areas is concerned. The development may also enhance the possibilities of collaboration between disciplines, which may counteract the traditional isolation of foreign language teaching.

On the other hand, language teaching cannot and should not leave the national orientation altogether. The languages have played a central role in the national development of the countries in question. Thus there are still important historical reasons for dealing with Denmark, UK, the United States, and France on the level of the nation-state (and below, studying social and cultural complexity). Moreover, there are good (non-linguistic) reasons for dealing with the large countries, namely their political, commercial and cultural position in the world today. In fact, all language teaching has to create a balance between an exclusive national orientation and a broader, maybe more universal, orientation.

Conclusion

This article is a sociological study of the theoretical basis of the teaching and learning of culture and language, and it primarily wants to criticize the still widespread idea within these fields that language and culture are inseparable. The article shows how language and culture may be disconnected in three different respects, and that they are reconnected in new relationships, one of the key concepts being recontextualization. Practice within the field of language teaching is already responding to some extent to these new configurations, but we are still waiting for a general theoretical discussion of the issue, which presupposes integration between the sociology of language focusing on multilingualism, and fields like macro-anthropology (cf. Hannerz 1992), focusing on multiculturalism and cultural complexity.

Notes

[1] A good discussion of the Herder-Humboldt-Sapir-Whorf tradition concerning the relationship between language, cognition and culture may be found in Schlesinger 1991.

[2] A slightly longer version of this article is Risager 1996b, which is in Danish.

[3] While at the same time many languages (and cultures) become extinct.

[4] I avoid the terms C1, C2 et etc. in order not to confuse with the term C1 meaning own culture and C2 meaning foreign culture or target culture.

[5] Murphy 1988 uses distinctions which in many respects resemble mine, but she does not focus on possible disconnections as I do.

[6] In this connection I mean by linguistic complexity the result of the fact that languages are put into contact with one another. This can be understood as a phenomenon of language use: the use of different languages or variants of the same language in the same or in an adjacent place (cf. Risager 1993), and as a phenomenon of language structure: the development of e.g. the semantics of the language through borrowing etc.

[7] But a topic may be treated differently in different cultures, because of differences in relevance structure.

References

Barth, Fredrik, 1989. The Analysis of Culture in complex Societies. In: *Ethos* 54.

Berns, Margie, 1990. *Contexts of Competence. Social and Cultural Considerations in Communicative Language Teaching.* New York and London: Plenum Press.

Byram, Michael, Carol Morgan and colleagues, 1994. *Teaching-and-Learning Language-and-Culture.* Clevedon: Multilingual Matters.

Byram, Michael and Geneviève Zarate, 1994. Definitions, Objectives and Assessment of Socio-cultural Competence. *The Council of Europe*, CC-LANG (94) 1.

Faerch, Claus, Kirsten Haastrup og Robert Phillipson, 1984. *Learner Language and Language Learning.* København: Gyldendal.

Fairclough, Norman, 1992. *Discourse and Social Change.* Cambridge: Polity Press.

Fishman, Joshua A., 1971. *The Sociology of Language: an Interdisciplinary Social Science Approach to Language in Society.* Pp. 217-404 in Fishman, Joshua A. (ed.), *Advances in the Sociology of Language I.* The Hague and Paris: Mouton.

Geertz, Clifford, 1973. Thick Description: Toward an Interpretive Theory of Culture. Pp. 3-30 in Cl. Geertz: *The Interpretation of Cultures. Selected essays by Clifford Geertz.* New York: Basic Books.

Halliday, M.A.K., 1978. *Language as Social Semiotic. The Social Interpretation of Language and Meaning.* London: Edward Arnold.

Halliday, M.A.K. and Ruqaiya Hasan, 1989. *Language, Context, and Text: Aspects of Language in a Social-Semiotic Perspective.* Oxford: Oxford Univesity Press.

Hannerz, Ulf, 1992. *Cultural Complexity. Studies in the Social Organization of Meaning.* New York: Columbia University Press.

Kachru, B.B., 1986. *The Alchemy of English. The Spread, Functions and Models of Non-native Englishes.* Oxford: Pergamon Press.

Kramsch, Claire, 1993. *Context and Culture in Language Teaching.* Oxford: Oxford University Press.

Murphy, Elizabeth, 1988. The Cultural Dimension in Foreign Language Teaching: Four Models. Pp. 147-62 in *Language, Culture and Curriculum* vol. 1 no. 2.

Preisler, Bent, 1998. Functions and forms of English in a European EFL-country. In Richard J. Watts and Tony Bex (eds.): *Standard English: The Continuing Debate.* London: Routledge.

Risager, Karen, 1996a. Language policy in practice. The language teacher and linguistic diversity in Europe. Pp. 20-29 in *ROLIG-papir 56*, Roskilde Universitetscenter.

Risager, Karen, 1996b. Sprog, kultur og internationalisering i sprogundervisningen. In Karen Risager (red.), *Sprog, kultur, intersprog. ROLIG-papir 57*, Roskilde University.

Risager, Karen, 1997. Language teachers' identity in the process of European integration: In Michael Byram and Michael Fleming (eds.), *Foreign Language Learning in Intercultural Perspective*. Cambridge: Cambridge University Press.

Robertson, Roland, 1995. Glocalization: Time-Space and Homogeneity-Heterogeneity. In: Mike Featherstone et al. (eds.): *Global Modernities*. London m.m.: Sage Publications.

Schlesinger, I.M., 1991. The wax and wane of Whorfien views. Pp. 7-44 in Robert L. Cooper and Bernard Spolsky (eds): *The Influence of Language on Culture and Thought. Essays in Honour of Joshua A. Fishman's Sixty-Fifth Birthday*. Berlin and New York: Mouton de Gruyter.

Williams, Raymond, 1988 (1st ed. 1976). *Keywords. A vocabulary of culture and society*. London: Fontana Press.

Wilson, Rob and Wimal Dissanayake (eds.): 1996. *Global Local. Cultural Production and the Transnational Imaginary*. Durham and London: Duke University Press.

The Problem of Identity in French-speaking Belgium

Inge Degn

That Belgium consists of two populations, who speak different languages, Flemish and French, is well known. When the Belgian State was created in 1830, the constitutional assembly chose one official language, French, and in one view the history of Belgium became one long struggle for the recognition of the Flemish language and culture. What outsiders often know less about or don't know at all, is that the French-speaking population is not just a homogeneous group, but consists of at least two main groups, the Walloons and the Brusselers. The individual French-speaking Belgian may thus define himself in relation to three levels: 1) in relation to the traditional, national level, i. e. as a Belgian, 2) in relation to the French Community of Belgium, i. e. as French-speaking, and 3) in relation to his region, e. g. as a Walloon. It is this complex reality and the questions of identity connected with it, which this article deals with.

The organization of Belgium

In what precedes I have already implied a complex structure, which refers to the political institutional organization of Belgium. At the latest constitutional reform, which was carried through in 1993, Belgium became a federal State, comprising three regions (Flanders, Wallonia and Brussels) and three communities (defined by their languages: Dutch, French and German), giving a total of four entities. After the elections in May 1995, Belgium has besides the federal Parliament (Chamber and Senate), five legislative assemblies, one for Flanders, one for the French-speaking Community, one for the Walloon Region (including the German-speaking municipalities), one for the Region of Brussels-Capital and one for the German-speaking Community.

This organization is clearly unequal, as the fusion of the region (Flanders) and the Flemish Community in the North provides a very simple structure centered around one pole, the Flemish Parliament and the Flemish government, while the network of institutions and political levels in the South constitutes a far more complicated structure with several poles.

The Flemish model reflects the fact that the Flemings constitute a very well-defined homogeneous group, largely characterized by a shared language, culture and religion and a clearly demarcated territory, while the model of the French-speaking seems to reveal a much more complicated relation between the component parts and levels.

Several opinion polls have shown that a large majority of the Belgians, both Flemings and French-speaking, want to remain Belgians,[1] and the popular mourning at the death of King Baudouin (1993) as well as the White March (Sunday the 20th of October 1996) have been interpreted by many as national manifestations. None the less the political debate is dominated by the question of a possible splitting of the country.

The debate on the future of Belgium is continuous, kept going by the calendar and the current political negotiations,[2] but it has been extraordinarily intense during the autumn of 1996, when it flared up as a result of the Belgian Parliament's reading of three framework laws on the „social security", the budget and employment. It was the Flemish wish for a division of the „social security"[3] that made this debate degenerate into a quarrel between the communities [4] and it finally made some French-speaking face the fact that Belgium migh some day come to an end.[5] Leading Flemings have set the legislative elections in 1999 as a deadline for new decisive reforms of the constitution with the object of obtaining greater autonomy for Flanders.

The Liège political scientist Marco Martiniello is among those who have analysed this situation. According to him, the political debate in Belgium is a disguise of a nationalist debate where the identity and ethnic discourse is prevalent.[6]

When characterizing the debate as not openly ethnic, Martiniello is hardly aiming at the Flemings, who declare themselves to be a nation.[7] He is more likely referring to the French-speaking, who are not clearly organized as a group, nation or *ethnie*, and who are reluctant to speak of this conflict as ethnic.

Martiniello also views the organization of Belgium as ethnic: the regionalisation and the creation of institutions according to the linguistic groups (Flemish-, French- and German-speaking) and the unilingual constituencies in Belgium express an ethnically structured political participation, and the policy that is conducted (language policy, territorial policy, distribution of ressources are determined by ethnic frontiers) contributes to a political construction of the ethnicity (Martiniello, 1995:61-63). However this is not an exhaustive description of today's French-speaking Belgium, which the above exposition of the institutional organization gives evidence of. The French-speaking collaborate on the communitarian level in the French Community, but the fact that they are divided between two regions, Brussels-Capital and Wallonia, a division that differentiates French-speaking Brusselers and Walloons, is not taken into consideration in Martiniellos presentation.

The corpus of the analysis

This is the background on which I decided to take a look on the French-speaking debate concerning the political institutions and the future of Belgium and its populations, looking for types of identy and identity discourses. In what follows, I am going to present some readings focusing on the attitudes and identities, their discourse and logic, expressed in this connection in the current debate. The material for the investigation is mainly the French-speaking weekly *Le Vif-L'express*[8] (Le Vif) covering a period of four months, from mid-July to mid-November 1996. But this material has been completed by supplementary material filling marked „gaps" in the discourse I have been dealing with. What we see is a field of movements caused by actions and reactions. The French-speaking respond, not only to the Flemish demands and pressures, but also to demands, criticism, attacks and questioning from others within the French-speaking field. Four major types of French-Belgian identity appear that I would not dare call ethnic in the sense that Martiniello defines it,[9] but sooner as an attitude to Belgium coupled with a specific selfcomprehension. These four identities are the Belgian, the French, the Walloon and the post-national or the European identies. Of these groupings only the irredentists speak for a dissolution of the Belgian State, while the remaining three are compatible with or even fight for the preservation of Belgium. The Belgian identity, in its extreme form sometimes called „belgicain", is attached to (identify with) the Belgium of 1830, the unitarian State. The apologists of the French identity conceive the French-speaking Belgians as naturally belonging to the French community or even *ethnie*, and want to return to France. The Walloon option gives priority to the regional level over the national. Martiniello himself is an exponent of the fourth attitude, the post-national[10] or European:

> *la construction d'une démocratie post-nationale et multiculturelle qui pourrait servir de modèle à l'Europe. Tant bien que mal, la Belgique a en effet jusqu'à présent réussi à combiner, sans coûts humains excessifs, les principes d'unité politique - certes relative - et de diversité culturelle. On ne peut que souhaiter que cela continue, en Belgique mais aussi ailleurs.*
> (Dieckhoff, 1996:104)

At first sight this attitude is related to a broadly accepted stereotype stating that the identity of the Belgian people is not to have any identity, and it is hardly a mere coincidence that it is often coupled with a criticicm of national identity, accused of being nationalist or ethnic.[11] This attitude is opposed by a clearly and strongly expressed Belgian identity.

The „Belgian" Identity

The Belgian discourse can be found on two different levels and under two different forms. The first is the affective discourse, the citizen, who in a letter declares his faith in the Belgian identity and in *la Belgique une et indivisible*, thus professing, in spite of the federalisation, the traditional Nation-State logic where the particular is transcended into the Nation.[12] The second is more philosophically based and anchors the relation to the State in the *citoyenneté*. While this conception sees the insufficient political participation in the modern society and especially in Belgium as the major threat against the survival of the state, the first considers any nationalism or regionalism, and above all the Flemish, as a threat to the continuance of Belgium:

> *En lisant votre hebdomadaire, j'ai l'occasion d'y découvrir (presque) chaque semaine un article concernant les actions que la Flandre fait pour accroître son indépendance. Etant abonné également à d'autres hebdomadaires, je ne puis m'empêcher de remarquer que vous êtes le seul qui soyez indignés ou même qui remarquez que la scission des maisons de tourisme à l'étranger, plus important, celle de la sécurité sociale, ou encore l'implantation du parlement flamand à Bruxelles (et j'en passe) conduisent la Belgique à sa perte. C'est en tant que Belge et fier de l'être[13] que je pousse le cri d'alarme. Il est temps que les francophones réagissent. Si nous voulons une seule Belgique où Flamands et Wallons vivent en paix et non en se battant pour obtenir la moindre petite miette de pouvoir, nous devons nous battre afin que la Belgique devienne un exemple de bonne entente entre gens de langue différente. Pour cela, je pense qu'il existe des solutions (comme implanter le parlement wallon ainsi que la Communauté française à Bruxelles) mais les politiciens francophones au pouvoir ont l'air de ne pas remarquer qu'en exerçant la politique qu'ils mènent actuellement, dans dix ans, Bruxelles sera flamand.*

> *L'Union fait la force n'étant plus applicable comme devise, acceptons au moins celle de la France qui dit Liberté, Egalité, Fraternité.*
> (E.S., Rochefort) (Le Vif, 19/7 1996:105).

This vision, where the image of Flanders as an enemy is clearly mobilising, and the not very subtle mixing of national uniting process and what might be called a French-Belgian nationalism are however only to be found in pure form, as in the example above, in the correspondence column. They also shine through, however, in Le Vif's editorials and certain articles, and in parts of the political discourse, cf. the leader of the French-speaking Liberal Party, Louis Michel, below. The position of the magazine is interesting, because it declares itself as a supporter of a united Belgium, but in the event of a final partition of Belgium, it considers a union with France a realistic and logical possibility.[14]

In the present situation, where the question of the relationship between the communities is boiling, Le Vif summoned two leading politicians in order to discuss this situation.[15] The two politicians were Philippe Busquin, leader of the Socialist Party and a Walloon, and Louis Michel, leader of the Liberal Coalition and a Brusseler. The agenda was set by the magazine, which has often pointed out the division of the French-speaking communities in contrast with the unity of Flanders.[16]

The magazine's question to the political leaders is how they are going to face the Flemish challenges and demands for more autonomy. The French-speaking politicians reject a partition of the state just like the readers in the correspondence columns,[17] so they go into a discussion of the institutions that regulate the relationship between the communities. Their conceptions of these institutions and the discourse that is used in the discussion show great differences.

A front of the French-speaking or a Wallonia-Brussels alliance?

The question asked by Le Vif is actually totally rhetorical: Must French-speaking Belgium take its destiny into its own hands?[18]

The liberal leader Louis Michel addresses the question by advocating a front of the French-speaking, because the Flemings take advantage of the division of the French-speaking. Michel would have preferred the merging of the French-speaking Community and the Walloon Region, but confronted with the socialist rejection of this, he tries to approach the socialist concepts of solidarity and union between Wallonia and Brussels by exchanging *front francophone* by *espace francophone*.[19]

Philippe Busquin refuses to relate to the problematic posed by the terms of Le Vif, preferring to talk about the level of the State: the reaction of the French-speaking must be grounded on the Constitutional State.[20] He develops the internal disagreement between French-speaking Belgians by referring to the Saint-Michel and the Saint-Quentin agreements in 1992. The late leader of the Liberal Party, Jean Gol, then spoke of a French-speaking nation, which the socialists dislike, because that would be to play the game of the Flemings and accept the particular to prevail over the universal.[21] The Socialists insist on the term of „nouvelle alliance Wallonie-Bruxelles" because it stresses the alliance between regions, and they do not want to be defined by the French Community, with which expressions like „espace francophone" and „front francophone" would inevitably be associated.

It can be concluded that while the Socialists see the transcending of the differences within Belgium as taking place in the Belgian Nation-State, the Liberals would want to form a French-speaking nation, which would transcend the differences between the French-speaking, and which could be effective in the battle against the Flemings. However the Socialists insist on the non-nationalist principle and refuse to mix the questions of identity and institutions. If the Socialists would wish to (re)construct an identity, it would in other words be regional. The liberal leader does not mention the word identity directly, it is only used in the related discourses by Le Vif and in the correspondence columns, but the identity issue is clearly at stake when he characterises the French Community as being „exsanguine", and his calling for a mobilising cultural and political project is at best ambiguous. At the same time he attacks the Walloon politicians for not having been able to create a mobilising project. This discourse exposes some of the historical, cultural and economic barriers between Walloons and Brusselers (Le Vif, 6/9 1996:49, cf. note 19).

Louis Michel has the last word in this discussion, calling for a sacred union between French-speaking Belgians: „Il faut une union sacrée entre francophones." (ibid:51)

The division on the French-speaking side reflects in fact a deep political disagreement on fundamentals between liberals and socialists, but also between Brusellers and Walloons. While the PRL-FDF, a coalition of The liberal Party and the Brusseler Federalists, would have liked to see a fusion of region and community corresponding to the Flemish construction, giving priority to the community dimension, the Socialists regard the region as the more important level, a clear signal that they weight the cultural and the political-economic-social dimension in a totally different way. The liberal message is clear, the Socialists' objectives are more vague, which also reflects divergences between the Brussels part and the Walloon part of the party and between the party on the federal level and the party on the regional level.

Though both parties maintain Belgium as their frame of reference, one feels the impossibility of a common project. However, what the Liberals want seems to be the appropiate answer to the attitudes expressed in Le Vif's correspondence columns.

A Vif discourse?

This image of Belgium transmitted by Le Vif can be completed through its dealing with the White March on Sunday the 20th October.[22] Paul Wynants, professor of history at the University of Namur, relates the march to the reaction at the death of King Baudouin. He sees the cult of the king and the gathering around the parents of the disappeared or killed children as a national manifestation implying a criticism of the politicians.[23] He emphasizes that these two events have not split the population in the usual groups, but that it acts as one body, and he continues that if the population realizes that it must invest in the State, a new *citoyenneté* might come into being.[24] Wynants, who is a Walloon, thus stresses the level of the State like Busquin. Others go further in conjuring up the image of a unitarian Belgium as one nation, as in the following statement: Sunday three barriers fell: the linguistic barrier, the ethnic barrier and the barrier between people and State. It was a beautiful image of Belgium.[25]

It is however highly problematic to imagine a „revival" of Belgium as one nation. The scission of the political parties has caused the Belgian political system to be deprived of its supreme judge, the „sovereign nation", which delivers its judgement at the elections.[26] The electors cannot express themselves as a nation any more, they have become groups of interest.

The propaganda for a French-Belgian project is taken up again in Le Vif 8/11 96, in an article stressing the necessity to present a clear image of Wallonia-Brussells to the outside, to satisfy the psychological needs of the French-speaking citizens to perceive a united French-Belgian society, and to see themselves as members of their community:

> *Au moment où la déliquescence de l'etat belge devient chaque jour plus évidente et où les francophones réalisent qu'ils risquent de se retrouver bientôt „Belges tout seuls", il est impérieux pour eux de se réunir autour d'un projet collectif mobilisateur. Car une communauté politique se forge en bonne partie par ses projets. (...)*

> *Comment donner aux partenaires étrangers de nos relations extérieures une image claire et cohérente de l'ensemble Wallonie-Bruxelles (...)?*

> *Les choix institutionnels, quant à eux, sont commandés tout à la fois par la volonté de la Flandre de s'ériger en Etat et par la complémentarité objective de la Wallonie et de Bruxelles. A quoi s'ajoute la nécessité psychologique, pour le citoyen, de percevoir une unité de direction de l'espace Wallonie-Bruxelles en gestation.*

Un débat sur le „contenu" des politiques doit permettre aux citoyens désorientés de se resituer comme membres de leur Communauté et, ultérieurement, d'adhérer, sinon au détail des solutions prônées, du moins au projet global et aux institutions qui le portent. (...)

Dans la perspective rapprochée d'une prise en charge de leur destin par les Wallons et les Bruxellois, un nouveau contrat social doit être mis en chantier toutes affaires cessantes. (Le Vif 8/11 1996:34)

Even though he speaks at the end of *un nouveau contrat social* and uses the word *citoyen*, one notices a slip from the State to the Community, from *citoyen* to member of the Community; *l'ensemble* and *l'espace* seem to be understood as something along the lines of a nation.

The opinion formers convened by Le Vif obviously want to replace the Belgian identity by a French Community identity. The latter does not exist, while the former obviously does. Some claim that if a Nation and a national identity were ever constructed in Belgium, they were Flemish (Verjans, 1995). But I think that we have to admit that the Belgian Nation was also constructed. The result was a nation symbolically and culturally constructed as a Belgian society on the French model. The nation created in 1830 corresponds to the *Staatnation*, it was the State, that created the Nation, and it was the French-speaking élite that imposed itself as the collective and individual model.[27] It is the result of this construction that we see in the correspondence column, and behind the editorial line of Le Vif.

The French Community and the Region have not been able to replace the Nation-State, and there have not been created any effective myths and symbols in connection with the Community and the Region. What counts is still Belgium, even though it has become federal.

The sense of belonging to the French Community and the Region is very different. As a matter of fact it is difficult to see the difference between the French Community and Belgium on the ideological level; both can be seen as a unitarian culture that strives to preserve Belgium including Flanders also, and for want of something better French-speaking Belgium. The problem of the region of Wallonia probably is that it has not yet become a success, and it is much easier to join a success than the opposite of a success. I am here speaking of the economic and social dimension, from which a shifting of identity can hardly be seperated.

With a little audacity one might assemble the *Belgian* considerations into a discourse stating that the division is caused by the institutions which have been created by the politicians. This is based on the conception that Nation and State should be concordant and they are not: The nation wants a united Belgium, the politicians (i.e. the State) just have to do what the people wants.

The Irredentists[28]

Another version of this Nation-State logic leads the populations of Belgium towards two other states, the French-speaking belonging naturally to the French *ethnie* or the French Nation. In his *Open letter to a Flemish friend, historian,*[29] the now retired Liège professor of History, François Perin, author of *Histoire d'une nation introuvable*, 1988, and an outstandig Walloon politician for decades, asks the question if, instead of maintaining their caricature of a State, it would not be better for Flemings and Walloons to turn to the neighbouring countries with which they share their languages and from which they have been separated by force.

The logic of this point of view is clearly ethnic as pointed out in a later issue of Le Vif:

> *(...) la solution du rattachement à la France: Cette „solution finale simple et claire", prônée notamment par François Perin dans son Histoire d'une nation introuvable, semble de loin la plus réaliste aujourd'hui: l'inté-gration économique entre la Wallonie et la France est déjà largement d'actualité, et l'identité historique, culturelle et ethnique commune est difficilement contestable.* (Le Vif 11/10 1996:56)

Judging from this selection of Le Vif-l'Express magazines, the „Belgians" and the irredentists get more attention, they are allowed to make themselves heard more than the Walloons, whose presence in this forum is negatively marked: a reproach for the failure to create a mobilising project and for giving the priority to the region.[30] What the Walloon politicians say in Le Vif has nothing to do with an identity discourse, except for the profiling in relation to the Flemings. No declared Walloon has expressed himself in the correspondence column; on the contrary, the attempt to construct a Walloon identity is repeatedly denounced as nationalist and separatist and is labelled *ultra*. There was hardly anything on the celebration of the Walloon national day in September. To see a more Walloon debate and identity discussion, one will have to look elsewhere. The explanation to this is given below.

The construction of a Walloon identity

Analysts often have to conclude, that the Walloon population suffers from a lack of collective consciousness. As a matter of fact its only point of reference, economically as well as socially and culturally, has been Belgium, and a Belgium where it was little known, where it has felt victim of stereotyped judgements, or ignored by the media and the schools.[31]

The official institute of culture of Wallonia, *Institut Jules Destrée*, and private associations like *Fondation Wallonne P.-M. et J.-F. Humblet* contribute to the (re)construction of a Walloon identity, essentially by uncovering the history of Wallonia. It is a problem that there has not been created a founding myth and effective symbols supporting the existence of Wallonia, although some claim that historical events like the National Walloon Congres (1945), the Royal Question (1950) or the Strikes of 1960-61 constitute founding moments in the history of Wallonia.[32] One notices that they are all recent historical moments illustrating the difference from Flanders. All serious endeavours to construct a Walloon culture and cultural identity end up with more questions than answers: will the Walloons adopt Wallonia, will the politicians and the Walloon Movement be able to create the necessary cohesion, what will the institutional frame of Wallonia be in the future?[33] Yet another example that cultural identity can be seen as an entity within different institutional frames, but that culture and cultural identity are not conceived of as determining the political institutional choice.

The post-national or European attitude

We have seen that Le Vif considers the division of the French-speaking Belgians as a weakness, which is used as a background for urging them to unite. Others view this as a potential: the Belgian construction as carried out by the French-speaking Belgians might be a practicable way for the organization of a multicultural society (cf. the vision of Martiniello above). This corresponds to the new type of nation where the nationality is dissociated from origin and cultural homogeneity.[34] Marc Quaghebeur from the Ministry of Culture of the French Community asserts the Belgian model as a new flexible model that will be able to deal with the problems in the new Europe: the European construction will have to solve problems concerning language and culture and their place and function when they do not coincide with a territory (Quaghebeur, 1993:53-54).

By operating a splitting up of the power into more levels, i.e. the State (abstract), the Region (territorial) and the Community (non-territorial, psychological, where the individuals share the community of language and culture), French-speaking Belgium has created a level of power between the state and the region, the function of which is to deal with culture and language (Quaghebeur, 1993:56). Quaghebeur's views are close to Martiniello's post-national

European vision (cf. above). This position denounces the nationalist and ethnic aspects of the identity debate. Unfortunatly, this image seems far from the Belgian reality, and the wish for a dissociation of the cultural identity and the political community, of Nation and State, might first of all bring French political thinking in mind as formulated e.g. by the French sociologist Dominique Schnapper: The political tradition in France has always refused the American conception of „ethnicity" (Schnapper, 1991:91).

Conclusion

The four „identities" that appear through these readings are all strongly influenced by the deficient stability of the Belgian institutions and denote different types of reaction to the loss of identity caused by the continuous reforms of the State and the draining of the Nation-State in Belgium.

The French-speaking politicians are left with an almost impossible task. The creation of the institutions (region and community) can be seen as an attempt to make people change identity by decree, which has not succeeded, and the politicians seem just as reluctant to the dismanteling of the Belgian Nation as their constituents. What has caused this situation, in the view of the French-speaking, is nationalism, the fact that the Flemings have let their ethnic particularity prevail over the common national political project. This is unanimously condemned by the French-Belgians. However, both the liberal discourse and the irredentism discourse do contain genuinely ethnic elements just as the Belgian „Belgicain" discourse must be characterized as nationalist. And the ascription of the ethnicity discourse to the Fleming, clearly pointed out as the „Other", is an ethnicisation of the political debate. The Walloon option and the socialist programme both strive to give priority to the region and/or the State as a political project over the cultural community. Despite these inner tensions, a Nation-State model closely related with the French Nation-State model is a common point of reference to all of them. The thinking pattern thus seems to be deeply culturally rooted.

For even though the debate, as it turns out in the columns of Le Vif, is marked by ideological and „regional" differencies, it shows a picture of a dominant French-Belgian attitude, which in general aspires to preserve Belgium. When Belgium's unity is attacked, two main reactions appear: one that refuses to consider/relate to the problem, and/or which calls for unity in a French-Belgian opposition to the Flemish demands, and one which insists on Belgium as a federal framework for political collaboration. (Irredentism is a special version of the former). One could say, that what you see is either a defense reaction confronting nationalism with nationalism, or a defense reaction that opposes a cultural understanding of the national with a political and rational understanding. While the former clearly represents a form of ethnic nationalism, the latter is more ambiguous in that respect. Theoretically it is beyond nationalism, but not inpractice. On the contrary one could think that they are sometimes internally connected.

The concept of a postnational identity, though radically different from the model that has been realized in France, is a return to the original ideas concerning the Social Contract. This is the ideal of the French republican model as it is still represented and defended by e. g. Dominique Schnapper. Historically this model has, however, de facto been destructive to different cultural identities in its French realization. In the Belgian context it has caused a strong Flemish nationalism, and this seems to be the explanation why the Walloon claiming of a specific identity has never had *droit de cité* in the Belgian nation.

Notes

[1]   Le Vif, 11/10 1996, p. 3. See also Robert.1994.
[2]   The Flemish national day on the 11th of July, the pilgrimage to the Yser/Ijser to commemorate the fallen Flemish soldiers during World War I at the end of August, the September declaration of the Van den Brande government and the federal negotiations on the budget, judging from what provokes comments in Le Vif.
[3]   Le Vif-L'Express 12/7:6.
[4]   Reacting to the Flemish wish for splitting up the social security system, the leader of the francophone socialists in the Chamber launched this threat: „Si vous voulez que la France se trouve aux portes de Bruxelles, alors allez-y!". (Le Vif 12/7:17)
[5]   In September four Francophone intellectuals published a manifest, Choisir l'avenir, which explicitly relates to this threat. The manifest caused some debate, but it only appears indirectly in Le Vif. (Le Vif 13/9 1996: 23)
[6]   Martiniello: „En Belgique, on déguise pudiquement le débat nationaliste en termes politiques et institutionnels. Et, lorsque les intellectuels crient „casse-cou", mettent en garde contre les dangers d'exclusion et dénoncent la violence intrinsèque du discours identitaire et ethnique, ils se voient répondre qu'"il ne s'agit pas de cela". Mais si!" (VIF 11/10 96, p. 56)
[7]   E.g. Louis Vos in Dumont e. al., 1989:203-220.
[8]   Le Vif is a francophone weekly closely connected with Paris, being the Belgian edition of the Paris weekly L'Express. It prints many articles dealing with this political debate, partly analyses, partly discussions, often arranged by itself, and in addition you often find letters in the correspondence column dealing with the institutions and the state of the country.
[9]   „Elle [l'ethnicité] repose sur la production et la reproduction de définitions sociales et politiques de la différence physique, psychologique et culturelle entre des groupes

dits ethniques qui développent entre eux des relations de différents types (coopéra-
tion, conflits, compétition, domination, reconnaissance, etc.)." (Martiniello 1995:18);
„[L'ethnicité] se définit plutôt par la croyance dans l'existence d'une continuité
culturelle qui caractériserait le groupe ethnique et par le sentiment d'appartenance
à ce groupe." (Martiniello, 1995:85)

[10] The term has been defined and discussed by the French philosopher Jean-Marc
Ferry (Ferry, 1991,2:191f; Ferry in Destatte, Jacquemin, Orban-Ferrauge, Van Dam,
1995:23-38).

[11] A. D'Haenens: „L'identité belge se cherche. Non pas qu'elle aurait à se renouveller,
parce que tombée en désuétude. Mais il en est ainsi quand il s'agit d'elle." Guido
Fonteyn: „Au fond, ce manque de sentiment national est notre plus grand vertu.
N'est-ce pas sur lui que l'on construira l'Europe, plutôt que sur un fondamenta-
lisme nationaliste à la Tatcher (sic!), ou religieux à la Walesa?" (L'Europe aujourd'hui. Les hommes, leur pays, leur culture. La Belgique. Un pays raconté par
les siens sous la direction d'Albert d'Haenens, Editions Artis-Historia, Bruxelles.
1991: 235 and 261).

[12] „La Belgique fédérale a encore de beaux jours devant elle. (...) Ce pays est un Etat
pluriculturel, plusieurs langues s'y côtoient, des traditions ont su y être préservées.
(...) Dans ce combat pour la préservation de l'identité belge, (...) Mettons fin à cette
surenchère communautaire. Les uns parlant de séparatisme, les autres de rattachisme.
Balivernes que tout cela en comparaison avec les problèmes de société qui secouent
notre pays. La Belgique sera toujours une et indivisible et ceux qui me prouveront
le contraire ne sont pas encore nés. (Paul Braconier, Bruxelles) (Le Vif 11/10
1996:144); cf. Schnapper, 1991:71.

[13] „Belge et fier de l'être" was the name of an association fighting for the preservation
of the unitarian State. At the federalization it changed its name into „La Fondation
belge" (Robert, 1994).

[14] Editorial: „Le Vif L'Express n'a jamais souhaité l'éclatement de la Belgique. Comme
la grande majorité de nos lecteurs, nous restons atachés à ce pays un peu artificiel,
né des aléas de l'Histoire, mais où la rencontre des mondes latin et germanique a
composé un art de vivre original et attachant." (Le Vif, 11/10 1996:3); „Celle [la
voie] d'une union à la France est la moins fantaisiste (...)" (ibid:16); „(cette solution) semble de loin la plus réaliste aujourd'hui." (ibid:56)

[15] Le Vif 6/9 1996:44-51.

[16] „Le 11 juillet est la date la plus symbolique: unie autour d'une seule institution,
alors que les francophones se dispersent entre la Région wallonne, la Communauté
française et la Région bruxelloise, la Flandre trouve là un moment propice pour
réfléchir à son identité. (Le Vif 19/7 96:17)

[17] Cf. the socialist Prime Minister of the Region of Brussels Charles Picqué (PS)
arguing on the example of Brussels that French-speaking and Flemings can
cooperate: „Personnellement, je me battrai pour sauver un fédéralisme qui repousse
la scission de la sécurité sociale, qui maintient la solidarité. (...) Je suis très attaché
à la dimension d'Etat-nation. J'y crois davantage qu'à l'Europe des régions, par
exemple. (...) Je reste attaché à la Belgique pour les valeurs qu'elle a toujours

incarnées. Un: la recherche inlassable du consensus social. Deux: la tolérance à l'égard des cultures et des communautés." (Le Vif 2/8 1996:10-12).

[18] La Belgique francophone doit-elle prendre en main son destin? (Le Vif, 6/9 96:45)

[19] Louis Michel (PRL-FDF): „Moi, je suis prêt à refuser aux Flamands de négocier une nouvelle réforme de l'Etat. Mais je ne suis pas prêt à refuser tout seul! C'est pourquoi je plaide depuis très longtemps pour un front des francophones. (...) La Flandre est devenue historiquement une nation; elle veut aujourd'hui s'ériger en Etat.(...) Le plus urgent, aujourd'hui, c'est de dégager un consensus entre francophones. (...) sur le terrain communautaire, les Flamands profitent actuellement du manque d'unité politique des francophones. (...) là où le PRL-FDF parle d'„"espace francophone", le PS parle de „solidarité" ou d'„"union""entre la Wallonie et Bruxelles". (...) l'élaboration d'un projet politique, économique, social et culturel pour la Belgique francophone.(...) _Un et indivisible, le PS veut-il maintenir définitivement la Communauté française?_ (...) je n'évoque plus la fusion entre la Communauté française et la Région wallonne. Bien que je pense qu'„on" a raté une chance et commis une erreur historique en ne fusionnant pas nos institutions. (...) La manière dont les institutions francophones ont été construites porte les germes d'une très grande faiblesse. Actuellement, les francophones sont toujours sur la défensive. (...) le monde politique wallon (...) n'a manifestement pas su dégager un projet mobilisateur. Le choix plus régionaliste du PS a un peu bétonné les institutions. Cette division intra-francophone est une faiblesse que les Flamands exploitent et risquent d'exploiter encore quand on discutera de l'avenir de Bruxelles. (Le Vif, 6/9 1996:46-49)

[20] Philippe Busquin (PS): „(...) la réplique francophone doit être fondée sur l'Etat de droit. Wallons et Bruxellois doivent faire l'analyse de leurs institutions actuelles, les faire fonctionner au mieux. Optimaliser ce qui existe. Il y a des liens à renforcer ou à établir. (...) Y a-t-il moyen de clarifier ce concept de nouvelle alliance Wallonie-Bruxelles, avec une Communauté française qui reste un lien institutionnel, mais dont la vitalité est due à de bonnes relations entre Wallons et Bruxellois? ... il faut discuter sur des concepts identiques." (Le Vif 6/9 1996:47-48)

[21] „Car elle donne l'impression aux Flamands que nous entrons dans leur jeu et répliquons à leur nation flamande." (ibid:49)

[22] Le Vif 25/10 96

[23] „A la mort de Baudouin, beaucoup ont redouté l'éclatement du pays. Indirectement, l'adulation du roi - tout comme l'engouement actuel pour les parents - va parfois de pair avec le procès fait aux politiciens." (Le Vif 25/10 96:15)

[24] Si la population comprend qu'elle doit réinvestir l'Etat, plutôt que de le laisser aller à vau-l'eau, le thème de la nouvelle citoyenneté peut devenir réalité. Alors, Julie, Mélissa, An et Eefje ne seront peut-être pas mortes pour rien. (Le Vif 25/10 96:15)

[25] „Dimanche trois barrières sont tombées: La barrière linguistique (...); la barrière ethnique (...); la barrière entre le peuple et l'etat (...). C'était une belle image de la Belgique (...)." (Le Vif 25/10 96:18)

[26] „(...) il n'y a plus, en effet, de „Belges" élisant leurs représentants, mais des francophones et des Flamands choisissant des responsables politiques de „leur" camp. Ce découpage électoral empêche l'arbitrage." (Le Vif 11/10:52)

[27] Cf. Juteau, 1994:60, on Canada; see also Schnapper, 1991:37.

[28] The Mouvement wallon pour le retour à la France (president: Maurice Lebeau), has about 750 members, among others François Perin. But this way of thinking seems to be much more widespread than indicated by the number of the devotees.

[29] „(...) allons-nous nous obstiner à maintenir cet Etat qui n'est plus qu'une caricature de nation (...). Quant à nous, Flamands et Wallons, ne devrions-nous pas nous tourner vers les nations voisines de même langue dont nous avons été écartés par la force à des époques où „les princes s'arrachaient les pays comme des ivrognes à la taverne se disputent les plats." (Marguerite Yourcenar, *L'œuvre au noir*, p. 17)." (Le Vif 19/7 1996:19)

[30] Cf. note 19

[31] Cf. Le Guide de la Wallonie:35-36.

[32] Cf. Wynants characterizing two of these moments as dividing: La Question royale, la guerre scolaire ou les grèves de 1960 ont, à chaque fois, réactivé les clivages communautaires, philosophiques, religieux ou socio-économiques (Le Vif 25/10 96:15).

[33] „Dans l'état actuel des mentalités, les éléments recensés [de l'imaginaire wallon] peuvent tout aussi bien s'agréger à une image wallonne que venir enrichir encore une image de la Belgique, une image de la francophonie belge, une image européenne et, pourquoi pas, diraient les irrédentistes, venir diversifier l'image d'une grande France. (Courtois and Pirotte, 1994:283)

Bibliography

Courtois, Luc et Jean Pirotte (dir.). 1994. *L'Imaginaire wallon. Jalons pour une identité qui se construit*, Louvain-la-Neuve.

Destatte et al. (eds.). 1995. *Nationalisme et postnationalisme*. Namur: Presses universitaires de Namur.

Dieckhoff, Alain (ed.), 1996. *Belgique. La force de la désunion*, Bruxelles.

Dumont, Hugues et al. (eds.). 1989. *Belgitude et crise de l'Etat belge*. Bruxelles.

Ferry, Jean-Marc. 1991. *Les puissances de l'expérience*, 1-2. Paris: Éditions du Cerf.

Fourier, Martine et Geneviève Vermès (éds.). 1994. *Ethnicisation des rapports sociaux: racismes, nationalismes, ethnicismes et culturalismes*, Fontenay/St. Cloud, Paris: L'Harmattan.

Le Guide de la Wallonie. 1994. Paris: Casterman.

d'Haenens, Albert (ed.). 1991. *L'Europe aujourd'hui. Les hommes, leur pays, leur culture. La Belgique. Un pays raconté par les siens sous la direction d'Albert d'Haenens*. Bruxelles: Editions Artis-Historia.

Juteau, Danielle. 1994. Multiculturalisme, inter-culturalisme et production de la nation. *Ethnicisation des rapports sociaux: racismes, nationalismes, ethnicismes et culturalismes*. Fourier, Martine and Geneviève Vermès (eds.)

Martiniello, Marco. 1995. *L'ethnicité dans les sciences sociales contemporaines*. Paris: PUF.

Quaghebeur, Marc. 1993. Pour une vraie pluralité européenne *Écriture et démocratie. Les francophones s'interrogent*, Coloque des 18 et 19 février 1993. Bruxelles: Labor.

Robert, Michel. 1994. *La Belgique dans tous ses états*. Bruxelles.

Schnapper, Dominique. 1991. *La France de l'intégration. Sociologie de la nation en 1990*. Paris: Gallimard.

Verjans, Pierre. 1995. Les clivages entérinés dans la constitution belge. *Agenda interculturel*, no 139, décembre 1995, p. 19-24.

Vos, Louis. 1989. Nation belge et mouvement flamand. *Belgitude et crise de l'Etat belge* Dumont, Hugues et al. (eds.). Bruxelles.

Yourcenar, Marguerite. 1968. *L'Œuvre au Noir*. Paris: Gallimard Folio.

Language Choice as Identity Construction in Pan-European Interaction – a Case Study

Jim O'Driscoll

Starting point

This paper reports on a study of the language choices and language attitudes in a multilingual educational institution. After brief reviews of the wider linguistic environment in which this institution is situated and the place of this study in language-choice scholarship, it explains how the data was collected and analysed and makes deductions from it. Given this essentially empirical procedure, a brief statement of my approach seems advisable. What has all this got to do with identity?

It is axiomatic in many branches and schools of linguistics (e.g. sociolinguistics, stylistics, pragmatics, systemics) that the 'meaning' of any instantiation of language goes well beyond the merely denotational, the purely cognitive-semantic. There are various types of this 'associative meaning' (Leech 1974:27) and they can be found at any level of the linguistic system, from the sound segment to the macro-textual. Most frequently, they depend for their existence on the possibility of paradigmatic alternatives – what would change if form X was substituted for form Y in environment Z. My position is that language choice operates as one such alternative. In any interactive situation where more than one language is, or seems to be, available, to participants, the use of one (hereafter Lx) rather than another (hereafter Ly) has meaning. Inter alia, it says something about the attitudes of the speaker towards him/herself, his/her interlocutor(s), the relationship between them and the situation at hand. Clearly, therefore, it has relevance for the concept of identity.

Languages in europe at the public/official level

The frame of this particular study is pan-European, where the notion of identity is a constantly salient subject in the context of the development of the European Union. And it is clear that languages, in their turn, are a constantly salient element in the identity question. To date, the EU's official approach has been very simple. Every language which has official status in a member state automatically becomes an offifical EU language as well.[1] The costs of this formal multilingualism have been well-rehearsed elsewhere (Coulmas 1991a, Lockwood 1994, Roche 1991). It is enough to note that no EU institution has so far made use of article 6 of regulation 1/58, which allows it to limit the use of the official languages in specific cases. In addition, where prescriptions for use of national languages have been made by national governments, the European Court tends to support them, even though they might be said to contravene community laws on free movement of persons, goods and services (De Witte 1991).

This association of Lx with member-state X is rigidly adhered to at formal EU meetings. In fact, there are signs that it has become more rigid than it used to be. Whereas in the 1970s, officials of the West German government showed willingness to recognize the de facto supremacy of English and French (Coulmas 1990), by the beginning of this decade their permanent representatives in the EU Commission were obliged by their government "to use German in all communications with the Community, to speak German at meetings, and to insist on documents of the meetings in German" (Ammon 1990:166). In 1994, it was reported (Lockwood 1994) that the German ambassador to the EU made a point of using German in all his official dealings even though his English was fluent. A nice example of the representative power of specific languages was provided in 1994 during meetings under the Danish presidency of the EU, when the Danish chair spoke English but the Danish delegation spoke Danish.

But what happens at the more informal level of everyday interaction among those working in pan-European institutions? Here, we may presume that personal and interpersonal aspects of identity are also a factor and that practical considerations demand that the purported equal status of all EU languages has to be ignored. It is here that we can find out how particular languages relate to identity for the individuals concerned.[2]

The research background

The multilingual mosaic of Europe has been a fertile ground for studies in several aspects of language contact. Broadly speaking, the research that has been conducted to date falls into two categories. On the one hand, there have been studies within the ethnographic and/or social-psychological traditions which focus on the attitudes and choices of people resident in particular localities (e.g. Denison 1971, Blom & Gumperz 1972, Trudgill & Tzavaras 1977, Gal 1979, Dorian 1987, Gardner-Chloros 1991, Jaspaert & Kroon 1991, Rampton

1995) and the identities which are evinced thereby. On the other hand, there has been macro-sociolinguistic work focusing on the roles of various languages in large areas (e.g. Trudgill ed. 1984, Ammon 1990, Coulmas ed. 1991b, Haarman 1990, Parry et al eds. 1994,) which explores notions such as numbers of speakers, language status, prestige and the use of languages in public domains.

Both of these types of studies have much to offer in the way of heuristic principles and theory-building. However, neither offers a precedent for the study of a pan-European multilingual community. The latter, 'macro', type does at least involve the interplay of a large number of languages, but it does not explore the relation of languages and identity in interaction at an interpersonal level.

The former, ethnographic, type addresses the question of identity but is on the wrong scale. All of these studies may be intepreted in the framework of essentially diglossic situations, involving a distinction between H varieties and L varieties (Ferguson 1959). Often only two varieties of language are involved, one of them the H standard variety of the wider social context, the other a more localized L variety (Blom & Gumperz 1972, Trudgill & Tzavaras 1977, Gal 1979, Dorian 1987). Even when more than 2 varieties are involved, their interplay is still in the context of one dominant H variety of the wider social context (Denison 1971, Gardner-Chloros 1991, Jaspaert & Kroon 1991, Rampton 1995).

The focus in these studies is thus on the relation of 'captive' communities to the big, bad outside world (Corrarubias 1983) – of 'ingroups' to 'outgroups'. Moreover, the emphasis is invariably on the captive community itself, this community and the outside world being conceived of as opposites. The studies thus tell us much about the effects of the outside-world on a community's habits, and any change is invariably presented as rapprochement to it.

In the European context, however, we need to take account of the language use and attitudes of speakers of 'majority' languages; something which Gorter (1994) notes is missing from present scholarship. The circumstances of language-ethnography in a typical captive community differ from those pertaining at a European level. The members of captive communities belong to it by inheritance and the community itself is defined by the (often long-standing) co-habitation of its members, usually in a clearly circumscribed geographical space. Members thus tend to have agreed norms of the attributes and symbolic value to be attached to various languages, and thus of the significance of using Lx rather than Ly and when it is normally appropriate to use each. In addition, there is a high degree of overlap in the repertoires of individuals in these communities, so that instrumental considerations play comparatively little part.

Bourhis (1979) has noted the lack of studies where groups may have conflicting norms of which choices are appropriate in particular situations. But it is precisely this situation which pertains in international interaction in modern Europe. With regard to repertoires and language use, the situation is not so much one of loss or maintenance of the captive community's language but rather the acquisition of lingua-francas added to existing repertoires. Ferguson (1982) has noted that language contact research has tended to ignore this development, and the concomitant development of giant speech 'communities'.

This study is in part an attempt to begin the filling-in of the empirical gaps noted above. It studies a micro-level speech community which may be said to be representative of a growing, new type of multilingualism. This community has coherence not by virtue of its members' permanent occupation of contiguous residential spaces but rather by virtue of its members' similar career orientation, backed up by their *temporary* occupation of contiguous residential spaces. The number of languages which different members of this community regard as their 'own' is very large, and most of these are H varieties in their 'own' territories. As such, its members originate from various speech communities with possibly diverging norms of use, so that the 'meaning' of the choice of Lx in interaction cannot be assumed to be the same for all those participating. In these circumstances, in addition to the overt, 'language-loyalty' type of conflict which can emerge in language choice, there is also the possibility of unmotivated conflict arising from misunderstanding of intentions. It is therefore a worthwhile enterprise, as a means of illuminating ideologies and outlooks, to attempt an understanding of how the available language choices are deployed in this kind of community and what speakers intend by their use.

The research site

Europa College in Bruges is a postgraduate institution which came into being in 1949 under the combined auspices of the post-war European movement, the city of Bruges and the Belgian province of West Flanders. Since 1990 it has had an annual intake of more than 200 students drawn from just about every country in Europe, and a few beyond. In November of the academic year 1993-94 (when this study began), the 266 students were from the following countries of origin (numbers from each in brackets): Spain (29); France (27); UK (26); Germany (25); Italy (24); Austria (12); Netherlands (11); Belgium, Ireland, Portugal, Sweden, Switzerland (9 each); Greece, Poland, USA (7); Denmark, Finland (5); Czech Republic, Hungary (4); Bulgaria, Canada, Roumania (3); Cyprus, Luxembourg, Malta, Russia, Slovakia (2); Albania, Bosnia, Croatia, Iceland, Mexico, Slovenia (1).

All students had been admitted to programmes of study in one of four departments: these were Law, Politics & Administration, Economics and the

Central and Eastern Europe Programme known as PECO (initials from its French name). Students stay at the college for one academic year, during which time they live in large residences belonging to the college. Nearly all are in their twenties. The academic staff is also multinational.

The official languages of the college are English and French and all courses are conducted in one or the other. Incoming students have to show documentation of ability in both languages before being accepted. Nevertheless, they are tested on arrival and several are obliged to follow remedial language courses.

The community at Europa College is thus similar to other modern organizations of a European scale in that its members have a multiplicity of geographical origin and 'native' languages, and they constitute an unusually highly educated elite. Students have normally obtained a top grade of first degree, and it is this academic record which has enabled them to get scholarships from their own countries. A few are sponsored by banks or diplomatic services.

On the other hand, this community is unlike other pan-European organizations in two ways. First, because the students share accommodation, their interaction involves a wider set of domains. Second, because they are temporary at the institution, we might assume that their dealings with each other are less circumspect than they are in organizations such as the EU Commission, where colleagues may have to get on with each other for years to come and where they might be competing for promotion.

In terms of representativeness, these dissimilarities may be an advantage. Since individuals members of this community do not stay together very long, we may presume they do not have the time to develop an ethos which is peculiarly their own and widely divergent from similar communities. In addition, there is likely to be less 'skewing' of the balance of languages than there can be in other institutions. At the EU Commission in Brussels, for example, the work of some directorates-general concerns particular areas outside the EU. We may suppose that, say, Russian is used in the DG which liaises with former COMECON countries to an extent which is unrepresentative of the Commission as a whole. At Europa College, on the other hand, interaction with outside bodies is irrelevant.

Research methodology

Fieldwork took the form of a survey-questionnaire given to all students, supplemented by informal observation and discussion with students. The items on the questionnaire which are relevant to this paper were multiple-choice (see table 1 for an example). Respondents were asked to pick out one or more of the (then) nine official EU languages, but with an opportunity to 'write-in' other languages. There was repeated encouragement to add comments. Two versions were sent, one English one French, these being identical in layout. A covering letter (also in two versions) asked students to complete whichever one they preferred.

This paper concentrates on the results obtained from the questionnaire. Since evidence for the reliability of self-reports of language use is mixed, some justification for reliance on these, as opposed to direct speech data, is necessary. It concerns the nature of the results which were desired. First, the plethora of ethnolinguistic identities among the student body means that it could not be assumed that the speech data gleaned from what would inevitably have been a very small proportion of the whole would be representative. Second, the aim was not primarily to estimate the roles of particular languages in an objective sense, but more to investigate the role of languages in identity construction. As such, the subjective data offered by questionnaire responses is at least as relevant as the language-choice data retrievable from examination of actual instances of use.

Language choice: the dyad item

Nevertheless, the depth of the overall picture is likely to be greater if the subjective responses provide a reasonable approximation to the reality of language use, if only because it allows information on attitudes to be interpreted within the framework of this reality. From this point of view, I claim that the responses in this study were more reliable than they are in many other questionnaire-surveys. This is because the items asking about language choice were framed so that one of the major introspective burdens on respondents in this type of exercise was removed. Respondents were NOT asked to indicate their language habits with TYPES of people (e.g. members of staff, people from Germany, people on the same course as me). Instead, they were asked about their habits with specific, named individuals. From lists provided by the college, students were grouped according to college-residence and study-programme. Each student was sent his/her own copy of the questionnaire. Page 3 (of 4) asked him/her to indicate his/her language habits with the fellow-students with whom, because they lived in the same residence and/or were studying on the same programme, s/he was most likely to have regular contact. (see table 1). It is claimed that introspecting on one's interaction with a known individual is much easier, and therefore one's response more reliable, than introspecting on interaction with an imposed category of person.

Table 1 exemplar of page 3 of questionnaire (English language version)

Think of the 8-12 fellow-students (eight to twelve – no more!) with whom you have the most frequent contact. What language(s) do you use to talk to each of them? If any of them do not appear in this list, please write their names in 17-20 below
1 Christina Boswell   DAN DEU ENG ESP FRA ITA NED POR
2 Anne-Charlotte Bournoville DAN DEU ENG ESP FRA ITA NED POR
3 Mark Callanan   DAN DEU ENG ESP FRA ITA NED POR
4 Asuncion Caparros Puebla   DAN DEU ENG ESP FRA ITA NED POR
5 Paula Alexandra Gaspar   DAN DEU ENG ESP FRA ITA NED POR
[[names numbered 6 - 16, followed by 17 - 20 with names left blank]]
If you use more than one language with the same person, what does your choice of language depend on? Please give as much detail as you can below (eg "with no.3 ... ")

This technique also provides a direct opportunity to assess reliability of responses. It means that respondent A's indication of his/her language habits with B can often be compared with respondent B's indication of his/her language habits with A.[3] When the returned questionnaires were analysed, cross-checking allowed two levels of results to be compiled: at one level, the pattern of all claims of language use, and, more restricted, a relatively objective set comprising only those cases in which respondents agreed.

Ethnolinguistic identity: the L1 item

Two other types of questionnaire item relevant to this paper are outlined here (others are mentioned in context later on). The first item on the questionnaire was used to establish linguistic identity as subjectively conceived. It went like this:

> *What do you regard as your 'native' or 'first' language' (e.g the first one learnt, the one in which you talk to yourself)? (IF YOU NEED TO CIRCLE MORE THAN ONE LANGUAGE, PLEASE ADD COMMENT HERE) Quelle langue considérez-vous comme votre langue 'maternelle' ou 'premièrè' langue (par ex. la première langue apprise, celle dans laquelle vous vous parlez à votre-même)? (SI VOUS DEVEZ ENTOURER PLUS D'UNE LANGUE, VEUILLEZ AJOUTER UN COMMENTAIRE ICI).*

The L1 concept can be variously characterized and indeed can be misused in research to reinforce dangerous misconceptions relating to ethnicity (Rampton 1995:336-344). Therefore, the rubric for this item was designed so that possibly conflicting characterizations would emerge. It includes implications of all the

possible meanings of L1: proficiency ('first language ... you talk to yourself/
langue .. première ... vous vous parlez B vous-même); inheritance ('native'/
'maternelle'); chronological acquisition ('first one learnt/première langue
apprise'); feelings of self-identification ('YOU regard as your 'native'/consi-
derez-VOUS comme votre langue 'maternelle' [capitals added here]). Thus,
the possible ambiguities of 'native/maternelle' (subjective identity or inherited?)
and 'first/première' (most proficient in or first learnt?) were turned to advantage
– if any of these concepts evoked different languages for the respondent, s/he
would cite more than one language and add comment.

In the event, very few divergences between expertize on the one hand and allegiance on the other (Rampton 1995:339–344) emerged. When they did,
allegiance, the more crucial to identity, was given priority, and in this way it
was possible to categorize nearly all respondents as 'natives' (hereafter L1ers)
of a single language.[4]

Respondent repertoires

In order to estimate the extent to which any one report of use of Lx by a respondent is a real choice and to what extent it is merely a necessity, it was necessary
to garner information about his/her overall language repertoire. The L1 item
contributed to this exercise. Other items did so not by asking about ability but
rather by asking about use. There is evidence that such self-assessments are
more reliable than those of ability (Gonzalez 1985). Of course, it may be argued
that they are still open to very varied interpretations. But for the purposes of
enquiring into identity construction, such unreliability is irrelevant; what matters is what languages people claim to use.

The EL versions of the repertoire items on the questionnaire were:
1 *Which language(s) have you used with relatives and/or friends in the past*
   12 months?
2 *Which language(s) do you use to deal with people in shops, cafés and offices*
   in Bruges?
3 *If you watch television here in Bruges, what language(s) is/are spoken on*
   the channel(s) you often watch?

Between them, these items thus covered the broad range of language-activity
types which have been mooted by scholars: both the interactional (1) and the
transactional (2) (Brown & Yule 1983:1-4); both the reciprocal (1-2) and the
non-reciprocal (3) (Widdowson 1978:57-76).

Preliminary analysis

191 completed questionnaires were returned, a response rate of 70%. No divergence was found between respondents and non-respondents with respect to any given category of identity (or with respect to proficiency in English and French as judged by college diagnostic tests). The quantifiable aspects of responses were entered onto a database, from which the figures in the following sections are drawn. Almost three-quarters of respondents added comments, and some of these are also cited in the following sections.

The results presented and discussed in these sections testify to a striking homogeneity among students at the college. Numerous pairings and groupings were tried in an attempt to find correlations between one category of 'given' identity and another. But remarkably few were found. That is to say, the overall pattern of language attitudes was broadly the same for each hall of residence, each department of study, each gender, and, until these were combined into vary large groups (see final section), each nationality and L1.

This general lack of departure from statistical theoretical distributions gives credence to the notion that the student body at the college is indeed a distinctive type of community, one with developing and norms and attitudes which operate irrespective of other kinds of group membership. The final two sections therefore concentrate on aspects of identity which seem to involve the student body as a whole.

Results: the promotion of a cosmopolitan identity

Table 2 is one way of rendering the overall pattern of claimed dyadic language use among students at the college. It includes only corroborated reports – that is use of Lx cited by both members of a dyad. As can be seen, only about 14% of these dyads made use of languages other than English or French, and less than a tenth made no use at all of either. Moreover, inspection revealed the vast majority of these latter to comprise L1ers of the same language.

Table 2 . Corroborated reports of language choices (total: 489)*

English only	186	French only	158
English + other language	9	French + other language	9
English + French	38	other language only	45
English + French + other language	2	(no agreement 40)	
Total dyads using English	235		
Total dyads using French	207		
Total dyads using another language	67		

Indeed, if fellow L1ers are omitted from the figures – as in table 3 – the relative absence of use of other languages is even more striking

Table 3. Corroborated reports: l1ers of different languages (tot:407)

English only	169		French only	140
English + other language	6		French + other language	6
English + French	38		other language only	10
English + French + other language	1		(no agreement 38)	
Total dyads using English		213		
Total dyads using French		184		
Total dyads using another language		22		

Most striking of all is (as further inspection revealed) the total absence of any language apart from English or French being used as a link language. Whenever interlocutors used a language which was neither of their L1s to interact, this language was, without exception, either English or French. In all cases, a reported 'other language' is the L1 of one partner in the dyad concerned. Among such a multilingual and educated population, I found this surprising. Even a depressingly typical non-ployglot anglophone as myself has had cause on occasion to use a language other than French as a link. Of course, the fact that English and French (hereafter EF) predominate as languages of everyday use at the college is not in itself surprising. But the overwhelming extent of this dominance, and the failure of other languages to put in a single appearance as a link language, provokes an attempt at explanation.

One obvious possibility is instrumentality. Perhaps most students do not see themselves as having the ability to communicate in other languages. However, the evidence from respondents' language repertoires does not support this hypothesis. Polyglottalism was much claimed among the student body. A third of respondents claimed non-L1 (hereafter L2) ability in at least one langauge other than EF, and analysis of dyads who were not fellow L1ers indicated that nearly a quarter had the potential to interact in such a medium. And yet only 5% of them produced corroborated reports of doing so (table 3). In addition, the format of the dyad questionnaire-item prioritises informal use (see previous section), so that it is unlikely that many individuals who claim ability in Lx also feel unequal to the task of dyadic interaction in this medium.

For the same reason – the highlight on informality – notions of appropriacy or of group solidarity can only furnish a part of the explanation for the dominance of EF. To some extent, it may be true that these languages are pressed into service so often as the result of students' desire to display their cosmopolitan credentials, their ability to be 'at home' in the high-powered world of international communication in which English and French are the established media, ratified as such by college language policy. From this point of view, students use EF on nearly all occasions because by doing so they affirm their full participation in college life, their membership of this international elite.

However, one can look at this the other way around. The very fact that these languages are established as the norms in this kind of environment, and are prescribed by the college, means that their use cannot have any interpersonal significance for interactants. They are merely default choices. Students must surely have desires not merely to belong to a group of 270-odd fellows, but also to forge more personal friendships. When they wish to predicate such interpersonal closeness, and they use language choice as a means of doing this, it would make more sense to use some other language whenever possible.

If we now look beyond corroborated reports and consider all claims of language use within dyads, the attempted use of non-EF languages becomes more evident. There were in all 1,523 reports of dyadic interaction between L1ers of different languages. 11% (172) of them claimed use of a non-EF language, which is double the proportion of such claims which were corroborated (table 3). A study of disagreements is also enlightening in this regard. Table 4 shows that, in dyads which did not consist of fellow L1ers, claims of EF-use were twice as likely to be corroborated as were claims of use of another language.

Table 4. Corroboration rate of lx-use claims: l1ers of different languages

	E	F	Other languages
number of claims of use in confirmed dyads*	529	484	95
number corroborated	426	368	44
corroboration rate	80%	76%	46%
* *confirmed dyads are those in which both members attested to their interaction*			

This partly explains the dominance of EF in the corroborated dyad figures above (tables 2 & 3). Other languages ARE claimed quite often, but only by one member of the dyad. We now need to ask why respondents disagree so much more often with respect to use of other languages. The answer may be indicated in an analysis of language-use claims according to the L1s of dyad-members. This shows that respondents more frequently claim the use of their interlocutors' L1 (552 claims in all) than they claim use of their own L1 (423 claims).[5] In Giles' theory of speech accommodation (e.g. Giles, Bourhis & Taylor 1977, Giles 1984), speakers converge to the language use of their interlocutors when they wish to identify with them. The pattern of responses here displays what might be called 'hyper-accommodation' (after the analogy of sociolinguistic hyper-correction), in the sense that this convergence often appears to be unappreciated.

It seems likely, therefore, that a significant part of the explanation for the overwhelming dominance of EF among students at the college is not merely their desire to use these languages but also their desire to AVOID using their L1s (with anybody except fellow L1ers), to avoid displays of ethnolinguistic identity. But when this is done by addressing alter in his/her L1, very possibly out of a desire to be friendly and polite, this friendliness and politeness cannot be reciprocated. Instead, it traps alter in the very kind of identity which s/he, like ego, is anxious to avoid.

It is a moot point as to whether such respondent disagreements indicate divergent perceptions of reality (A claims they both use Lx with each other while B claims they both use Ly with each other) or whether they indicate the same perception of failed attempts to impose Lx and Ly respectively as the medium of interaction (A uses Lx but B refuses to go along with this choice and uses Ly instead). It is quite possible that they could indicate both. But either way, it indicates a conflict of identity construction. Dyad members of different L1s tend to wish not to be addressed in their own L1s. When their interlocutors, who must have some awareness of this reluctance (since they partake of it themselves), do this, they cannot be said to be accommodating. The principle motivation for such behaviour may not be to converge to the perceived ethno-linguistic identity of interlocutors. What seems to be really important for students is to DIVerge from their own ethnolinguistic identities.

Given a prevalent attitude towards languages in general which presumes that code use among interactants ought to be symmetrical, it seems that, in these circumstances of identity-conflict, the use of EF emerges as a compromise solution to the problem, in which identities can be reciprocated and neither party is especially disadvantaged by being saddled with an identity that they would rather not advertise. This is an intriguing reversal of the oft-cited reason for the development of lingua francas in multilingual states – their neutrality value. The use of English in public life in places such as India and West Africa is explained by the idea that it avoids the unfair advantage that would be given to any one ethnolinguistic community within the state if their L1 was employed. But in the case of the multilingual community examined here, neutrality seems to be a matter of avoiding the unfair DISadvantage in which speakers of any one L1 would find themselves if their L1 were employed.

In suppport of this interpretation, it may be mentioned here that in comments appended to the returned questionnaires, the respondents who complained most vociferously about the perceived dominance of English at the college (see next section) were English L1ers. For example, one politics student wrote:

> [people] *basically answer any questions that I put to them in French, in English. At this stage, I have given up on even trying, as I just get so annoyed that the dominant language in the college is English ... . And then people wonder why the Irish and the English don't have good French: it is not through lack of trying!!! They might as well not bother calling the College of Europe a bilingual college*

L1ers of the dominant language are at a de facto disadvantage in an atmosphere in which the kind of identity which is accorded the highest value is that which asserts freedom from the constraints of ethnicity. It is this perception of English dominance which is addressed in the next section.

Results: French as a marker of elite identity

English hegemony in Europe

This section examines the balance of reported use of English on the one hand and French on the other and attempts to evaluate its significance. In terms of college language policy, the two co-exist on a level playing field. But in the wider European and global milieux, it can be safely stated that they do not. The greater importance of English in several fields of international activity is by now beyond doubt. This is most obvious in the leisure industry. There is no French equivalent of MTV. It is true that popular music in the French language may often be heard around Europe, but songs in English are simply inescapable in any corner of it (including France – see Flaitz 1989). In the summer of 1994, I conducted surveys of the written messages on the casual clothing worn by passers-by in the town-centres of Bruges and Limburg (Westphalia). Discounting brand or place names, more than 95% of all legible words were English.

The same picture of English dominance emerges when we examine book publishing (Flaitz 1989), academic conferences (Ammon 1990, Coulmas 1990), figures for enrolment in language-learning courses (McCallen 1989, Ammon 1991) and international broadcasting (there is no French language TV station with the broadcast capacity of CNN).

English hegemony within the college

This bias in favour of use of English in international contexts is reflected in several aspects of the returned questionnaires. For instance, it was recognized by respondents in their replies to an 'instrumentality' item, the EL version of which read:

> *Apart from your native/first language, which 2 languages do you con-*
> *sider the most useful for your (future) children to know (please indicate*
> *order of importance)?*

While not a single respondent failed to cite English here, a small but significant number rejected French, and more than three times as many respondents cited English as the language of primary importance.

The responses to another item on the questionnaire also indicate that English is regarded as more suitable when dealing with the wider world. This was the 'student-stranger' item, in which students were asked to indicate which language they normally used when addressing someone who (EL version) "you do not recognize but who you feel sure is a fellow-student". Around three times as many respondents claimed to use English as claimed to use French.

Moreover, many of the comments appended to responses to this item show evidence of a general perception of English as dominant. A quarter of respondents who use mainly English explained their occasional use of French as a desire to practice it; three respondents explained their use of French as a desire to redress the perceived imbalance towards English in the college. This perception also comes across in general comments added elsewhere on the questionnaire form. For example, one FL1er studying law wrote:

> *Le français est géneralement une seconde langue etrangère et moins*
> *facilement utilisé par les personnes qui ne sont ni de langue maternelle*
> *français, ni de langue maternelle anglaise.*

One EL1er (also a law student) wrote: 'Mes impressions au collège sont qu'il est plus anglophone que francophone'.

It would seem that most students are more comfortable with English than with French. The explanations given for the use of English with student-strangers never exhibited the strategic motivation noted above for use of French. Instead, ease of use was most commonly cited. Further evidence can be found in the language which was chosen as a medium of response to the questionnaires. Of those respondents whose choice was considered meaningful,[6] more than half as many again responded in English (42) as responded in French (26).

The lack of English hegemony in dyadic interaction
Given all of the above, the English/French ratio in dyads, as reported in responses, is somewhat startling. As table 5 shows, this ratio shows only a slight bias towards English, and remains broadly the same whichever sets of measurement are used (varying from ratios of 52:48 to 58:42).

Table 5 Comparative figures for reports of use of English : French

Corroborated reports	all	total use	235 : 207
		sole use	186 : 158
All reports	all	total use	1152 : 944
		sole use	710 : 518

In their comparatively high degree of French use as reported in dyadic interaction, the students of Europa College seem to be atypical of international communication in Europe as a whole. This level is also significantly higher than what general respective levels of proficiency among the student body might predict – and higher than what the students themselves would estimate. The deduction to be made from these apparent contradictions is that a large proportion of the student body, as was suggested by some of the explanations for using French with student-strangers (see above), makes a conscious effort to use French. Other respondents comments bear this out. For example, in commenting on the student-stranger item, a German PECO student wrote:

> *At the beginning of the academic year, I would have spoken English automatically. However, as I noticed that most students try to speak French, I would follow their example .... I want to improve my French – I am forcing myself to speak as much French as possible.'*

A Croatian student wrote that although 'I can express myself better in English than in French', 'for the majority of cases where the other person is good at French we speak French'. English, she writes, is used only 'with people that have difficulties with French'. French, it seems, is the language of aspiration. EL1ers are especially keen to practice French (see end of previous section). Moreover, FL1ers sometimes take part in this enthusiasm. One EL1er, commenting on the history of her interaction with an FL1er, wrote that:

> *'she began to think I assumed she would make the effort to speak English, and therefore made me speak French more!'*

One FL1er, commenting on her habits with both a British and a Spanish fellow student, wrote that they normally spoke English together except when working on a course taught in French and 'quand j'essaye de les faire parler francais un petit peu'. She reported exactly the same pattern with another British interlocutor, French being used only 'quand c'est pour pratiquer (explicitement) son francais'. On the other hand, English is the language of default. The desire to practice it is rarely mentioned in respondent comments.

At one level, the urge towards French may be explained as simply the seizing of an opportunity to make up for perceived deficiencies in foreign-language proficiency in general and/or a deficiency in a tongue whose acquisition has great instrumental value. However, the clear dominance of English in the wider world means that this value is limited and that therefore instrumentality is not in itself an adequate explanation. We also have to account for the fact that FL1ers themselves contribute to the promotion of French, even though this behaviour conflicts with the general tendency among students to avoid the use of their L1s (see previous section). It seems that the French language is held in particularly high esteem. In terms of Bordieu's (1977) notion of linguistic capital, it has a higher currency value than English.

Part of the reason for the relatively high value attached to French is its associations with 'high culture' and learning. Perhaps the image of English has been debased somewhat by its modern association with popular culture. One Slovak respondent, commenting on her language choices with members of the academic staff, wrote:

> *'English is more simple. French is more "continental". It is more appropriate to my way of thinking'.*

French appears to be 'classier' than English. As such its linguistic forms are more to be revered. An EL1er, explaining code switching with two FL1ers, wrote that 'somehow their incorrect English is more acceptable than my incorrect French'. The fact that one Hungarian explained his use of French with an FL1er by noting that 'he's very tolerant with non-native French speakers' might suggest that others are not so tolerant. This was articulated by one EL1er:

> *'En revanche je crois que les francophones tolerent moins les erreurs de français des autres que nous les tolerons en anglais'*

She had filled in the questionnaire in French for practice and 'veuillez excuser mes fautes!' It is reasonable, therefore, to see the drive towards French among people who hope to become the future European elite as a desire to identify themselves with a language which has elite associations. In classic diglossic terms (Ferguson 1959), French is the H variety and English the L variety.

At the same time, however, nobody could fail to acknowledge the contribution of English to 'culture' and learning. One of the very few respondents who evinced a desire to practice English alluded to the language of Skakespeare! The H/L distinction cannot, therefore, be pushed too hard. I would suggest that a further and fuller explanation can be found if we pursue the notion of linguistic capital, but revise it slightly by regarding different languages not as liquid assets (as implied by the term 'currency value') but rather as solid assets. As such they partake of the law of supply and demand. From this point of view, we can see that in present-day Europe, the greater value attached to French, and therefore to the possession of its forms, is not merely a matter of its perceived 'intrinsic' worth but also because of its comparative rarity. The 'supply' of English is very high. Everybody knows some, and many people know a lot (or think they do, which is what matters here). As a result, its unit price is low. The supply of French, on the other hand, is limited. Fewer people know any, and very few indeed know, or think they know (because it has such rigorous standards – see above) a lot. It has a much higher unit value.

The hypothesis that this outlook is an important aspect of the drive towards French finds support if we examine the dyad-language-use claims according to geolinguistic regions of origin. Table 6 enumerates all such claims.

Table 6. All reports of dyadic use of English : French between L1ers of different languages by respondent origin

Mediterranean L1ers*	290 : 197	= ratio 60 : 40
Northern L1ers**	300 : 234	56 : 44
Eastern L1ers***	104 : 160	39 : 61

* =	L1ers of Romance languages other then French and Romanian, plus Greek and Maltese.
** =	L1ers of all Germanic languages except English, and also Finnish.
*** =	L1ers of Slavic languages plus Albanian, Hungarian and Romanian.

The remarkable thing about these reports is that they are the opposite of what both received wisdom and the occasional survey would predict. It is 'common knowledge' that English is far more current than French in northern Europe, while in southern Europe its hegemony is less complete and French is often the better-known L2. The students themselves abide by this knowledge. In explaining his language-choice with student-strangers, one Danish respondent wrote:

> *'I use English as a rule; however if I reckon that the receiver has a more "latin" outlook, I would be inclined to use French'*

Another, a Croatian PECO student, indicated English as her normal choice with student-strangers but added: 'sometimes I use French if for some reason he or she looks like more "southern" European'. Conversely, one Spanish student 'usually address[es] fellow students in French' but 'tend[s] to address Scandinavians in English' because 'I know they'd rather speak in English'. This perceived divergence between north and south, however, is not reflected in the figures for claims of language use in table 6.

In Eastern Europe, English is thought to be making headway both against Russian and against German. A number of studies have mentioned this development (e.g. Ammon 1992) and various other scraps of evidence point the same way.[7] In all these reports, French gets hardly a mention. As a lingua franca in this region, it would seem to be in fourth place. And yet the preponderance of French use in dyads among East L1ers at Europa College is undeniable (see table 6).[8]

In summary, it would appear that the value of French to students at the college increases in proportion to its rarity in their home environments. French distinguishes the possessor of its forms because most people do not possess it. The students of Europa College, the next generation of the European elite, are naturally keen to possess the accoutrements (sic!) of their projected status.

Final remark

The evidence evaluated in this article suggests that languages continue to be employed in identity construction in Europe, even when freed from ethnolinguistic constraints. The specific deductions made here are, at the time of writing, being tested by a repeat study of students at Europa College for the year 1996-97 and a study of interaction among the students of the Central European University in Budapest. This time, encouraged by the high degree of apparent homogeneity of attitudes among students the first time, the study includes more personal ethnographic work and direct speech data is being gathered. It is hoped that this will add depth to the examination of motivations begun in this article.

Notes

1 The exception to this rule is Irish, which is a special case in that, while being the 'national language' of Ireland, it is the native speech of only a tiny fraction of the population, English being the native speech of everybody else. Even so, Irish still appears on documents such as driving licences and in court judgments.

2 It is indicative of the delicacy of the 'language question' at an EU level that attempts to research everyday interaction at institutions such as the EU Commission or Council of Ministers in Brussels are not encouraged. I spent years trying to set up research at the EU Commission. But I got nowhere. It was almost as if the offering of assistance to such research was a subversive act. In response to one of my enquiries, an informant of mine, a language specialist, chose to phone me rather than write because of the 'delicacy' of the matter in question. He said he thought it better not to commit

pen to paper and expressed the wish that he would not be named as the informant since the information he was giving was not sanctioned by the commission.

3 Not always, because sometimes two respondents do not cite each other from the list of names available, or because one of the students is a non-respondent.

4 Less than 10% of respondents claimed to be bilingual. In half these cases, the claim was rejected because allegiance was clearly to a single language. Only eight respondents were judged bilingual in analysis, and in calculations relating to L1ers, they were counted twice. (Two apparent trilinguals were omitted from the figures.)

5 This is not an artificial effect produced by the fact that there are fewer L1ers of EF than the sum of L1ers of all other languages. If EFL1ers are excluded, there are still significantly more claims of use of alter's L1 (90) than of ego's L1 (62).

6 It will be remembered that students were sent the questionnaire in both languages. It was considered that the mere fact of a respondent choosing to fill in the form in Lx rather than Ly would not in itself be significant – they might be equally comfortable in either language. So each student's questionnaire package was folded in such a way that one of the languages was 'prompted' (both the covering letter and the form itself in that language would be encountered first, and the respondent would be able to fill in the form in that language on the inside of the fold). It thus became possible to record those respondents who 'dispreferred' the prompted language and chose to respond in the other one.

7 For example, at the NELLE General Assembly in Maastricht November, 1991, it was reported that Poland needs 30,000 more English teachers and had 20,000 unwanted teachers of Russian. See also Medgyes & Kaplan (1992) for a Hungarian-based study.

8 At first, I thought these figures were some peculiar effect of the circumstances. Most East L1ers were enrolled in PECO. Perhaps French was promoted by staff in this department. Perhaps all courses were taught in French. But enquiries found neither to be the case. Moreover, one of the college language teachers told me that the same preponderance of French use over English use among eastern European students was apparent in the academic year following the survey, so that the figures do not appear to be an accident of the language preferences of a few strong personalities.

References

Ammon, U. 1990 German as an international language. *International Journal of the Sociology of Language* 83:135-170.

Ammon, U. 1991 The status of German and other languages in the European Community. In Coulmas (ed) 1991b pp 241-254.

Ammon, U. 1992 The Federal Republic of Germany's policy of spreading German. *International Journal of the Sociology of Language* 95:33-50.

Blom, J. & Gumperz, J. 1972 Social meaning in linguistic structure: Code-switching in Norway. *Directions in Sociolinguistics: The Ethnography of Communication*, Gumperz & Hymes (eds) New York: Holt, Rinehart & Winston pp 407-434.

Bordieu, P. 1977 l'Économie des Échanges linguistiques. *Langue francaise* 34.

Bourhis, R. 1979 Language in ethnic interaction: a social psychological approach. *Language and Ethnic Relations*, Giles & Saint-Jacques (eds) Oxford: Pergamon pp 117-142.

Brown, G. & Yule, G. 1983 *Discourse Analysis* Cambridge: Cambridge University Press.

Cobarrubias, J. 1983 Ethical Issues in Status Planning. *Progress in Language Planning*, Cobarrubias & Fishman (eds) Berlin: Mouton de Gruyter pp 41-85.

Coulmas, F. 1990 The status of German: some suggestions for future research. *International Journal of the Sociology of Language* 83:171-185

Coulmas, F. 1991a Introduction to Coulmas (ed) pp 1-43.

Coulmas, F. (ed) 1991b *A Language Policy for the European Community: Prospects and Quandaries* Berlin Mouton de Gruyter.

Denison, N. 1971 Some observations on language variety and plurilingualism. *Sociolinguistics*, Pride & Holmes (eds.) Harmondsworth: Penguin pp 65-77. (original full version in Ardener (ed) *Social Anthropology and Language* London Tavistock.

De Witte, B. 1991 The impact of European Community rules on linguistic policies of the Member States. In Coulmas (ed) 1991b pp 163-177.

Dorian, N. 1987 The value of language-maintenance efforts which are unlikely to succeed. *International Journal of the Sociology of Language* 68:57-67.

Ferguson, C. 1959 "Diglossia" *Word* 15:325-40.

Ferguson, C. 1982 Foreword to *The Other Tongue: English Across Cultures*, Kachru (ed.) Oxford: Pergamon.

Flaitz, J. 1988 *The Ideology of English* Berlin De Gruyter.

Gal, S. 1979 *Language Shift: Social Determinants of Linguistic Change in Bilingual Austria* New York: Academic Press.

Gardner-Chloros, P. 1991 *Language Selection and Switching in Strasbourg* Oxford: Clarendon.

Giles, H. 1984 (ed) *The Dynamics of Speech Accommodation.* International Journal of the Sociology of Language 46.

Giles, H., Bourhis, R., & Taylor, D. 1977 Towards a theory of language in ethnic group relations. *Language, Ethnicity and Intergroup Relations*, Giles (ed.) London: Academic Press.

Gonzalez, A. 1985 Language use surveys in the Phillipines (1968-1983). *International Journal of the Sociology of Language* 55:57-77.

Gorter, D. 1994 A malcontent from the village: a comment on John Edwards. *International Journal of the Sociology of Language* 110:105-111.

Haarmann, H. 1991 Language politics and the new European identity. In Coulmas (ed) 1991b.

Jaspaert, K. & Kroon, S. 1991 Social determinants of language shift by Italians in the Netherlands and Flanders. *International Journal of the Sociology of Language* 90:77-96.

Leech, G. 1974 *Semantics* Harmondsworth: Penguin.

Lockwood, C. 1994 Three more tiers could topple Europe's shaky tower of Babel. in *The Sunday Telegraph* 27/11/94:p29.

McCallen, B. 1989 *English: A World Commodity.* London: The Economist Intelligence Unit.

Medgyes, P & Kaplan, R. 1992 Discourse in a foreign language: the example of Hungarian scholars. *International Journal of the Sociology of Language* 98:67-100.

Parry, M., Davies, W. & Temple, R. 1994 (eds.) *The Changing Voices of Europe* Cardiff: University of Wales Press.

Rampton, B. 1995 *Crossing: Language and ethnicity among adolescents* Harlow: Longman.

Roche, N. 1991 Multilingualism in European Community meetings – a pragmatic approach. In Coulmas (ed) 1991b pp 139-146.

Trudgill, P. 1984 (ed.) *Language in the British Isles* Cambridge: Cambridge University Press.

Trudgill, P. & Tzavaras, G. 1977 Why Albanian-Greeks are not Albanians: language shift in Attica and Boitia. *Language, Ethnicity and Intergroup Relations*, Giles (ed.) London: Academic Press.

Widdowson, H. 1978 *Teaching Language as Communication* Oxford: Oxford University Press.

Do National Cultures Always Make a Difference?

Theoretical Considerations and Empirical Findings Related to a Series of Case Studies of Foreign Acquisitions of Danish Companies

Anne-Marie Søderberg

1. Approaches to cultural analysis

Even though analyses of the significance of cultural differences in connection with companies' internationalization is still a relatively new investigative field, it is an area that is now widely recognized as important by both practitioners and theoreticians, in principle at least. In many ways, culture has been increasingly in focus in recent years, both in the social debate and in applied business economic research, for example in connection with management, organizational studies and marketing.

Culture is being put into words, and cultural differences are becoming part of social discourse. But consensus about what we are to understand as culture has become even more difficult to achieve. And it is no less difficult to find ways to investigate and analyse cultures and cultural processes of change.

The classic anthropological culture concept, which has increasingly gained ground in humanistic, sociological and business economic circles during the past 10-15 years, is a concept that has become gravely problematical and eagerly deconstructed within the field of anthropology during the same period (cf. Hannerz, 1992 and Liep & Fog-Olwig, 1994).

In the classic perspective, which came into being with anthropological research in the 1950s and 60s, culture is perceived as something the members of society have and bear as something shared. They are socialized into a given culture that is handed down from generation to generation as collective meaning homogeneously distributed in society. If culture is perceived as something relatively static, an *empirical category*, culture analysts can explore culture, observe behaviour, ask individuals about their attitudes and values, systematize the data and define the characteristics that make a certain culture distinctive.

Within this approach it is thus assumed that it is possible to discover the core culture (the basic assumptions or culture patterns) as something objectively existing and identifiable.

Cultures are perceived in principle as compact wholes, clearly distinguished from other cultures and marked by sets of rules, regularity and predictability. This perception is connected to the idea of the nation or the national state as a community of people united by the same language and culture. It also has its basis in functionalism, which regards the single parts of culture as parts of a whole, each with its necessary function for maintaining and stabilizing the whole.

With a basis in a view of culture as an empirical category, a *form and substance system* (Hastrup 1989) which can be objectively delimited in time and space, culture is perceived as a psychological system that exists objectively in the psyche of the culture-bearer. This entity can be found by analysis, through registration and systematization of people's behaviour, which is assumed to be determined by their attitudes and values. This approach is thus concerned with the relationships between basic assumptions, values and their visible representations in artefacts and actions. Culture thus constitutes a type of „text", which the cultural analyst can *read* and interpret in order to draw up hypotheses about the underlying „cultural grammar", the system of rules of play that unconsciously control cultural practice.

The classic concept of culture as an *empirical category* and *a form and substance system* has been queried (cf. Hannerz, 1992, and Barth, 1994a). In recent anthropological studies this concept of culture has been abandoned for a perception of culture as a *system of relations* and an *analytical implication* (Hastrup 1995, p. 17).

If culture instead is perceived as an analytical implication, this in contrast implies that what we call culture comes into existence in relation to and in contrast with another culture. Culture is regarded as a social construct. The cultural data are constructed on the basis of the researcher's own cultural assumptions, and with the concepts and categories the researcher uses to systematize his or her experiences. The abstractions that can be produced by cultural analysis are indeed derived from observed patterns in the communication and behaviour of a group of people. However, within this approach the cultural analyst is aware that one cannot observe and describe another culture without taking with one a reflection of one's own cultural perspective, one's cognitive interests and the culturally determined tools one use for sensing and cognition. In this perspective culture is perceived not as something the individual *has*, but on the other hand as a fellowship that *is created between people and by people*. Culture is consequently the meaning people produce and shape in their contacts with one another in order to *construct* a coherent image of their world. Cultures is consequently something that anthropologists *construct* and *write* in order to establish some kind of order in their experiences of 'otherness' (van Maanen, 1988).

Within this approach to culture as an analytical implication it is thus emphasized that it is only possible to approach culture with concepts and analytical categories which in themselves are tools developed as a result of a culturally-determined interest for reflection on cultural differences[1].

Social reality has at the same time contributed to undermining the classic anthropological perception of culture as a static phenomenon, and as a homogeneous and well-delimited unity. A stable and consistent culture, where there is consensus among the members of the culture about knowledge, behaviour, attitudes and norms. A social community of the kind previously described in many anthropological field studies of an island society, or a closely interwoven, almost isolated, tribal society, is hardly ever encountered today, no matter where in the world one is. And as regards the old anthropological descriptions, it can indeed be discussed whether the consistency in the account might not be due to the anthropologist's (unconscious) desire to be able to describe a coherent cultural system, where order and stability prevailed.

If we just keep to Europe, it becomes increasingly difficult to maintain the national-romantic perception of Europe as a patchwork of local cultures, where the boundaries between local cultures follow the national boundaries. „The patchwork" has always been a theoretical abstraction. But the ideas about the uniformity and coherence of national cultures, ideas built up during the last 150-200 years in pace with the processes of forming nations and inventing national cultures, are increasingly disputed. Partly because of the political and economic integration in Western Europe, and partly because boundaries have been abolished or shifted, especially in the most recent past, when the Berlin Wall collapsed, the Iron Curtain rusted and unions of states disintegrated. At the same time, the building up of new national and ethnic collective cultures also helps to illustrate the fragility of the cultural constructions.

At the same time there has been a great migration of labour from the South to the North and from the East to the West. And this migration, together with the great number of refugees, has helped to make European society increasingly multi-cultural and at the same time has helped to put culture as a concept on the agenda and to accelerate the discussion about which cultural differences make a difference.

The internationalization of the economy and politics, as well as the migration and the extension of world-wide communication systems, has had the effect that ever increasing numbers of people no longer primarily define themselves by their affiliation to a geographic locality (a town, a region or a nation),. A place where they have „roots", and a language that is their „mother tongue". This applies in particular to the many people who today live in so-called transnational cultures. These are people who are employed in multinational companies, international organizations and research institutions, or who are connected with the diplomatic service or perhaps an international news service agency. It is in a certain sense a prerequisite for them that, to be able to work and be comfortable, they learn new methods of handling social constructions of meaning. Communication strategies that deviate from the local clusters of meaning and ways of managing meaning in which they were originally socialized (cf. Hannerz, 1990).

Anyway, the cultures that we find today in societies all over the world are extremely complex and dynamic. We are in a situation where the culturally specific in our experiences and forms of action on the one hand is becoming increasingly evident in many different spheres. And, on the other hand, where it is becoming increasingly difficult to define and delimit what we mean when we talk about culture. This is the point of departure for the theoretical reflections above.

The first thing to establish is that, in a modern multicultural society like the Danish society, the idea of one coherent and uniform culture within the boundaries of the nation seems by now inadequate. Instead we must perceive cultures as dynamic, marked by continual changes and contradictions. And consequently, we must be aware that people have a plurality of different perceptions and strategies within the framework of the nation. People create and develop a large number of cultural communities, local, national and transnational, and define themselves in relation to these. These cultures can represent values, attitudes and forms of behaviour that are mutually incompatible. So this sharing of culture is, in principle, only *situational*; it does not necessarily go beyond certain contextual circumstances. The cultures that are constructed and developed within a given society are not therefore unequivocal and uniform entities either, but on the contrary, they might be complex, heterogeneous and equivocal.

I have now briefly outlined some differences between the classic cultural concept from anthropology and the perception of culture that is today gaining a strong foothold in modern anthropology. The discussion in the theory clarification part of the research project has largely been centred on the zone of confrontation. Between on one hand anthropology as a general science of culture, and on the other hand comparative management and organizational culture; two different areas in organization and management theory which both reflect on cultural differences and their consequences. In the following I will look at the way different approaches to cultural analysis have been used in organization and management theory. In this connection I am only interested in identifying broad tendencies and so will not go into detail about differences between individual researchers in each of the two approaches I will look at more closely:

• analyses where culture is regarded as a variable
• analyses where culture is regarded as a socially constructed inventory of meanings

The two approaches also represent a chronological development in the science of anthropology, even though there are some temporal overlaps. For a closer characterization of the two approaches see Gertsen, Søderberg, Torp (1998).

2. „Cultural contacts and foreign acquisitions" - a research project

While a lot of research has been done in recent years on the export and investments by Danish companies in foreign markets, little is yet known about how foreign companies act in the Danish market. The number of foreign acquisitions of Danish companies has increased remarkably during the last decade. About 130,000 Danes are now employed in foreign-owned companies, which corresponds to 10% of all employees in the private sector. Developments are thus moving towards a situation where a large and steadily increasing proportion of the Danish workforce will come to work for large foreign concerns. And so they will be faced with the need to act within the strategy of the multinational company, and the need to be able to communicate with employees and managers in other business units.

No research has been done about what changes occur in the organization of the Danish companies and with their cultural identity and self-image as a result of the change to foreign ownership. Likewise, little research has been done on what form cultural contacts assume in encounters between the foreign owner and the acquired Danish company, internally in the company or in relation to the world around the company.

The Department of Intercultural Communication and Management at Copenhagen Business School decided to focus some research efforts on the issue *cultural differences as a managerial condition.* This enabled my colleagues, Martine Cardel Gertsen and Jens Erik Torp, and me to start an interdisciplinary project[2] on *"Cultural Contacts and Foreign Acquisitions"* in 1994.

We expected that, during the integration process, the owners, managers and employees in the foreign company would be confronted with conscious and

unconscious values, attitudes and forms of action, as they are expressed by the
Danish employees in the company, the customers, and other contacts in Danish
society. Like other researchers within the field of mergers and acquisitions we
expected that the daily life in the workplace after the acquisition would be
characterized by cultural contacts or even culture clashes. In fact there is an
amount of studies focusing on how to prevent serious cultural confrontations,
and how to predict difficulties related to an integration of different organizational
cultures. Cf. the book titles: Sales & Mirvis, 1984, *"When Cultures Collide:
Issues in Acquisitions"* and Altendorf, 1986, *"When Cultures Clash: A Case
Study of the Texaco Take-over of Getty Oil..."*[3]

In the project we defined cultural contacts as contacts between different
organizational cultures and different national cultures, as they are expressed in
intercultural communication processes between the employees and the companies.

However, our research project differed from most of the related projects described in the literature on business economics, by wanting to analyse both
contacts between different organizational cultures and between the national
cultures in which they were originally embedded. Typically, cultural research
within business economics concentrates on the national cultural dimension (in
the field of comparative management, where studies compare two or – generally – more nations for the purpose of isolating culturally determined differences
in the way management is practised). Or they focus on the company and the
organizational cultural dimension (in cultural studies of organizations within
the same nation).

We decided that the empirical part of the investigation for the moment would
be directed at the acquisition of Danish companies by foreign companies in the
field of electronics. In this branch, there have in fact been a large number of
acquisitions by foreign companies in the last decade, and, in addition, a number
of different nationalities (USA, UK, Germany, France, Norway, Holland, Belgium, South Korea) are represented among the take-over companies (cf. Gertsen, Søderberg, Torp, 1995).

We established contact with seven selected companies and made interviews
on the level of top management, in order to make an explorative analysis of
their experiences with cultural contacts between foreign and Danish companies.
In addition, we interviewed engineers and technicians, sales staff, secretaries
and skilled and unskilled workers in production. In order to illustrate the company's interaction with the local milieu, we also interviewed trade union leaders
and representatives for the local trade council as well as liaison organizations
between the university and the business community.

We visited the companies three times, in December 1994, March 1995 and April 1996. In this way we got the opportunity to observe the integration processes, over time and at a certain distance. However, the project cannot be regarded a longitudinal study, only as an attempt to give "snapshots" of how the employees interpreted their situation at certain moments.

In this article I want to discuss two issues:

• how to use various culture-theoretical and discourse-analytical approaches in the study of culturalcontacts and intercultural communication in foreign acquisitions in Denmark
• how to analyse companies´ and employees´ ongoing quest for cultural identities.

3. Culture as a variable: the functionalist paradigm

If you look at research in comparative management, you will probably note that the perception of culture as an independent variable has been very influential. The researcher who is probably the most renowned in this field of research, is Geert Hofstede (1984). He was greatly inspired by some American anthropologists who dominated anthropological discussion in the 1950s and 1960s, particularly Kluckhohn and Strodtbeck (1962) as well as Inkeles and Levinson (1954), whose suggestions for cultural universals, „standard analytic issues", correspond with Hofstede's cultural dimensions (Hofstede 1984; p. 37):

• *power distance*
• *uncertainty avoidance*
• *individualism versus collectivism*
• *masculinity versus femininity*

In addition to these, Hofstede later added a fifth dimension: *short-term contra long-term life orientation* (cf. Hofstede 1992), which is presumed to be particularly relevant when Asian and Western cultures are to be compared.

Hofstede defines these cultural dimensions as aspects of a culture that can be *measured* in relation to other cultures. Hofstede asserts that what is in question are basic value orientations that are present in all cultures, where the differences then represent the different solutions that cultures (= nations) have to the collective human problems. They should thus be cultural universals, even though Hofstede does not postulate that his cultural dimensions are in any way exhaustive.

Hofstede's concept of culture is based on the idea of „mental programming" of the individual, who is equipped with some particular patterns that fundamentally influence his way of thinking, feeling and acting (Hofstede 1991, p.

16). Mental programs according to Hofstede are mental structures that determine our conduct and our way of perceiving the world. With the programming metaphor taken from the computer world, Hofstede presupposes a perception of the person as a passive being, who is given an cultural input that determines behaviour by the socialization process. This view of people as cultural products is completely in tune with the idea that influences the so-called process school in communication theory, where the receiver is correspondingly regarded as a passive object for influence through text and speech (cf. for example Søderberg and Villemoes, 1994). If a person throughout his childhood and youth is „programmed" with particular values and attitudes, then the person is perceived as a „culture-bearer", a person who carries around and articulates particular cultural values and norms.

Values are the fundamental components in the mental programs; they constitute the nucleus of culture. Hofstede (1984) accordingly defines culture as follows:

> *„Culture is the collective programming of the mind which distinguishes members of one group from another"* (p.21).

For Hofstede, culture is thus primarily a system of collective behavioural-determining values, as it were, a group's „personality". The cultural values help to determine how the group reacts to its surroundings. Hofstede uses his culture definition on nations, organizations and small groups of every kind. In Hofstede (1992) the conceptual apparatus is used in connection with comparative studies of organizational cultures.

Trompenaars' investigations (1993) are yet another example of extensive empirical studies, based on value- oriented anthropological theory. Even though this is not explicitly stated, Trompenaars uses, in almost identical words, Parsons and Shils' suggestions for the cultural universals, which they have called „pattern variables":

- *Relationships with people*
  - *Universalism versus particularism*
  - *Individualism versus collectivism*
  - *Neutral or emotional*
  - *Specific versus diffuse*
  - *Achievement versus ascription*
- *Attitudes to time*
- *Attitudes to the environment*

Hofstede, Trompenaars and many other researchers in comparative management (cf. Ronen's overview of the subject, 1986) try to infer common national features in the way people act, think and formulate rules and norms for their

own and others behaviour from interview statements and answers to questionnaires.

This line of thought, which is the basis of Hofstede's and Trompenaars' research, implies the idea that people broadly shape themselves according to the
demands and expectations of their surroundings. They develop personality
characteristics and ways of acting in accordance with a particular regional or
national character. But such an idea about a national or regional character is
problematic, since, in principle, it is difficult to combine with a perception of
people as active producers and constructors of culture. When it is claimed that
everybody shares the same culture, then the individual can be anonymous, a
nobody.

Cultural analysis in this research tradition is influenced by a search for general elements, for regularities, which can be used to *predict* future behaviour, for
example a particular management style based on particular values. Comparative
management research is therefore very much in favour with multinational
companies and organizations.

Quantitative methods are frequently used in comparative cultural studies,
although it is not here claimed that there is a mechanical connection between
the choice of either a positivistic or a hermeneutic paradigm, and the choice of
a culture concept and a methodology for cultural investigation and analysis.
Measuring cultural differences, or describing such differences, is to enable
comparison between many cultures on a uniform basis. In this effort, culture is
reduced to an *independent variable*, a background factor in relation to the
company, on account of the fact that the company functions in a particular
cultural = national context.

Nevertheless, a problem with the measurement/description of cultural differences is that the cultural analytical models used are perhaps not general at all.
On the contrary they can represent the author's (unconscious) effort to project
his own (culturally determined) perception of the world onto other groups, so
that instead there is a form of ethnocentric conceptualization of cultural
differences. Hofstede's cultural categories are based on the concept that it is
possible to dichotomize every universe, which reflects a way of thinking, which
has dominated western philosophies and ideologies since the Enlightenment.[4]
In Hofstede's binarism a culture therefore must be feminine or masculine,
individualistic or collectivist, egalitarian or hierarchical. This simplistic way of
thinking overshadows any attention to how people in a specific context choose
their communicative strategies, and how people handle a specific communication
situation with regard to both the content and the relational aspects.

The risk of ethnocentric projection exists of course in every cultural analysis.
But it is greater when a pre-determined general model is used in a questionnaire

investigation. In this connection, it should be mentioned that Hofstede's and Trompenaars' *universalistic* ambition has also become questioned as problematical in the current anthropological discussion on scientific truth and validity and the conditions for producing valid knowledge on cultural differences (cf. Hastrup 1992). Also the idea that there is an unequivocal connection between people's expressed values and what they actually do has been disputed in both sociology and modern anthropology, (cf. Barth 1994b).

As I have shown, Hofstede and Trompenaars, who dominate current research on comparative management, build on the basis of a line of thought developed by American anthropologists in the 50s and the beginning of the 60s. Thus, there seems to be a sort of time lag, when we look at the concept of culture that this branch of management literature has chosen to use. As mentioned above, this classic culture concept has meanwhile been abandoned by the majority of anthropologists in favour of understanding cultures as social constructions of meaning, as an activity in which the actors and the communication process are taken seriously.

The functionalistic approach has inspired a number of theoreticians in the research field of organizational culture, too. Here, company culture is regarded as the values that the members of the organization have in common. These values can be expressed in cultural artefacts and in myths, rituals, language codes and in narratives telling the history of the company.

In studies of „corporate culture", organizational culture is often regarded as consisting of a collection of variables, and precisely value orientations are what are typical. It is assumed that these values are very susceptible to influence from top management. „Corporate culture" is therefore seen as an instrument that can help to ensure effective fulfilment of the strategic goals set by management. It is also taken for granted that an organizational culture should preferably be as homogeneous as possible. This is taken as an expression of its strength and contextual power. Subcultures within an organization are consequently regarded as hindrances in relation to fulfilling the goals of the organization. Striking advocates for this *integration perspective* (Martin, 1992) can be found among some of the authors who helped to spread the concept of corporate culture and make it popular in a company context: Peters & Waterman (1982) and Deal & Kennedy (1982) (cf. section 5 in this article).

In functionalistic organizational culture research, culture is seen as a closed system, where every single element has a function in the whole. Organizational culture is regarded as a system of values held in common, which serves important functions. Culture is a mechanism whose primary function is to *integrate* the organization internally and to *adapt* the organization to its surroundings.

Organizational culture should thus help to give coherence to the company internally, so the social system is stabilized. Organizational culture should give the employees an identity so they feel part of a larger group and consciously work at strengthening this group by various actions. Organizational culture should also help to adapt the company to its surroundings so the company can survive changing demands and expectations. The company should therefore mark its distinctive character in external communication to its competitors and customers.

In the functionalistic perspective organizational culture thus can be seen as a „consensus creating, normative 'glue'" (Schultz, 1995, p. 22), which can be influenced by the management so that the survival and efficiency of the organization is ensured as well as possible. The functionalists do not reject the existence of subcultures, but it is still the integrating role of culture that they emphasize. They are less occupied with internal contradictions, paradoxes and complexity.

4. Empirical findings related to national differences

On the basis of Hofstede's questionnaire studies and other comparative studies concerned with intercultural and international management questions, it may easily be assumed that when a foreign concern buys a Danish company, national cultures may play an important role, both in negotiation and purchase phases, as well as in the subsequent integration process. It is obvious too, that managers and employees in the companies expect that national differences can cause difficulties in communication, co-operation and integration. These expectations also influenced our way of thinking about the main issues to be investigated in the research project *"Cultural Contacts and Foreign Acquisitions"*.

Let us have a look at whether national differences played an important role in the cases we have investigated, and how these differences appeared. Our interviews with managers and employees show that strategic and economic considerations are predominant in the negotiation phase. Nevertheless, considerations about expected cultural differences and similarities could also be an issue. Some of our interviewees mentioned that they had been worried that problems could arise if the acquiring company was situated in a country where the culture was perceived as very far and different from the Danish culture, for example Japan and Japanese culture. So the concept of 'cultural distance' played a certain role among our informants.

Hofstede assumes that integration between companies imbedded in different national cultural settings is the more difficult the more distant the cultures are on Hofstede's scales of cultural dimensions. At first it sounds reasonable, but this assumption is not supported by our cases. Interviewees in a Danish company, which was first acquired by a British company and afterwards by a Korean company, told us that they experienced co-operation with the British employees as much more difficult than the co-operation with the Koreans. One explanation could be that the employees prepare themselves and make great efforts to overcome any difficulties in communication with people with a cultural background that is perceived as very distant from and strange to their own. Therefore they tend to show greater tolerance towards difficulties appearing in such intercultural communication processes. In co-operation with a company Danes perceive as 'close', whether Norwegian, British, German or American, they tend to expect the communication to be without friction and effort. When as a point of departure you tend to discount perhaps small cultural differences, for example in certain cultural assumptions and rhetorical strategies, these differences might have unintended consequences for communication and co-operation.

Such an explanation could give support to the statement that it is not sufficient to have an "objective" measurement of the closeness or distance to a certain national culture, in the form of a certain numerical value or a position on a certain scale showing a cultural dimension. Such a measurement can function as a kind of indicator that there may be difficulties in this dimension of the intercultural communication and co-operation. But for successful cultural integration between two companies, it might be just as important, or even more important, that the co-operating partners are open-minded, tolerant and able to act with flexibility and empathy when problems arise in the intercultural communication process.

With our interview data as access to the integration process in the company, we can only state that our interviewees relatively seldom refer to differences between (what they perceive as) national cultures as an important explanation of difficulties they have experienced in the company after the foreign acquisition.

This might indicate that it is much more difficult than assumed by Hofstede and other researchers within the field of comparative management to show clear correspondences between certain cultural values and people's behaviour in specific intercultural communication situations. There may not be the expected unequivocal correspondence between explicit value statements and (verbal) actions.

If national cultural differences do not play an important role as an explanation of difficulties in the integration process, this might also have to do with the fact that cross-national co-operation between companies is not co-operation between people deeply rooted in isolated national cultures. On the contrary, intercultural in internationally oriented companies, and who are involved in professional discourse about for example product development, financial control systems, management issues, and sales and marketing issues. This is not to say that national cultures never make a difference. It is only a statement which can used as a launching pad for new reflections about which cultural differences make important differences, and how you can describe these differences.

Nevertheless, there were some comments in the Danish companies which foreign managers and employees repeatedly expressed in interviews. These were some characteristics that certainly attracted their attention on the background of their experiences in their home country, characteristics that from their point of view made the company a Danish company. (Cf. the distinction made in section 1 in this paper on culture as an empirical category vs. culture as an analytical implication and theoretical construction).[5]

The power position of the Danish unions and the role they play in Danish companies are one of the issues mentioned by the foreign managers and employees. The other Nordic countries with long social democratic traditions have similarly powerful unions. But foreign managers from Great Britain and USA were not accustomed to the well-established position of the trade unions in society, nor the high degree of unionization. It was new to them to work at working places where not only the blue collar workers but also the secretaries, the technicians and the engineers were unionized to a great extent. The fact that local representatives of the trade unions participated in negotiations with the management of the company about general wage agreements and working conditions was a great surprise to them. Another surprising issue was the fact that it was not enough that the company negotiated with the individual employees, but that the company had to pay their employees a minimum wage according to fixed wage rates negotiated by trade unions and employers' associations.

Some of the foreign managers and employees working in the Danish companies were quite disconcerted when they realized that employee representatives were members of the board of directors. At first it was difficult for them to understand why these employees participated in the meetings, what role they played, and if it was possible to discuss any serious issues in their presence. Of course some of the foreign managers and chairmen of the boards reacted by transforming the board of directors into a formal setting, while all serious discussions and decisions were taken in a smaller executive committee where the employee representatives did not have access.

On the other hand, several foreign managers have said that they gradually gained a more positive view of the Danish trade unions and their representatives in the company. When the initial problems of understanding on both sides were overcome, they had noticed that Danish trade unions were broadly disposed towards co-operation and consensus, and that they were greatly interested in the company's welfare and economic success, as long as it could guarantee their members' continuous employment in the company. This attitude of the Danish unions was perceived as very much in contrast to the experiences with British and American trade unions, where the relations to the companies were characterized as uncompromising and conflict-oriented.

Danish employees' attitude to work – and especially to working hours – is another issue mentioned by some foreign managers in interviews, especially those expatriated from countries where the rate of female employment is much lower than in Denmark. The foreigners did not mention any problems in relation to the Danish employees' qualifications and job motivation. But they were surprised that Danish employees left the company at a fixed hour even if they had to leave tasks unfinished. Their surprise was great especially when this also happened among groups such as engineers working on a development project or among office staff in a human-resource management department.

I assume that one explanation for these observations made by the foreigners is the Danish family model, where both men and women have full time jobs, even when they have small children. The average age of the employees in the case companies was about 30 years. So many of the employees were parents to small children and share the duty of bringing the children to and from day nurseries and kindergartens, go shopping and prepare the meals. The reactions of the foreign managers may also reflect generation differences in lifestyle and attitudes to work and family life.

5. Empirical findings related to differences in organizational cultures

A majority of the researchers concerned with cultural aspects of mergers and acquisitions have focused on differences in organizational cultures. Cartwright and Cooper have undertaken one of the largest investigations within this field.[6] They base their book on a broad questionnaire study with 150 interviews, 600 questionnaire responses, and in addition, observations in a number of companies over a four-year period. All their cases are about horizontal mergers/acquisitions, which have needed large-scale integration.

Cartwright and Cooper are interested in the "cultural fit" of the companies. They recommend that a prior study is made of whether the cultures "match". As will appear from the following, the two organizational cultures do not have to be very similar for the acquisition or merger to become a success. But they should be able to act together, and that is why the cultures should be examined in advance. Even though the phases before the purchase are often long – 2 years is not unusual – the buyers, according to Cartwright and Cooper, know very little about the culture in the company they acquire. The financial aspects and the synergy potential as regards the products or the market, in contrast, are nearly always well examined. Cartwright and Cooper recommend that it should also be ensured that there is a cultural fit between the two organizations. A cultural analysis done prior to the purchase should make it possible to identify problems and then prevent them in the integration process. Or the culture fit-analysis should simply lead to the conclusion that the organizational cultures of the two companies are incompatible and that the acquisition/merger should therefore not be tried. The authors also point out, though, that the management of the integration process is important. Even though the chances for cultural adaptation are deemed to be good, the result can be a failure if the inte-gration process is managed badly – and vice versa.

Cartwright and Cooper have developed a simple culture typology, a univers-alistic tool, which they suggest decision-makers should use to describe orga-nizational cultures, even before making their decisions on acquisitions.

Cartwright and Cooper´s culture typology

Power culture:
In this culture, a distinct centralization of power is seen. It is often a question of small companies; often with a charismatic leader. Decisions are made by ma-nagement alone; often based on intuition. The reward systems are based on the personal preferences of the management and the employees have few challenges.

Role culture:
Here there is a case of a bureaucracy, where logic, rationality and efficiency have pride of place. What are important are functions rather than people, and division of labour is highly specialized. There are many rules and clear limits for work areas and authority. The hierarchy is formalized and clear to all.

Task culture:
The primary emphasis is on the actual tasks to be solved. The nature of the tasks determines the way one works. The organization is characterized by flexibility, autonomy and creativity. The tasks are challenging, but the employees run the risk of burning out.

Person culture:
The organization is egalitarian and the structure is minimal. The growth and development of the individual is regarded as the most important factor. The decisions are collective and all information is shared.

Comprehensive integration is usually needed in mergers. Here Cartwright and Cooper believe that the distance between the two cultures is important. They should preferably be adjoining types, because both companies normally want to retain their own culture.

With acquisition, there is generally a question of a type of situation where the acquired company is expected to adapt. The acquiring company on the other hand typically intends to retain its own culture. Cartwright and Cooper assert that the important thing in this situation is not the distance (the difference) between the cultures, but the question of the direction in which the autonomy is affected: is the freedom of the individual increased or decreased? If the employees experience that their autonomy is increased, the integration process will usually go well. Conversely, a reduction of the freedom of the individual creates problems. Cartwright and Cooper thus believe that the outcome can be predicted by plotting the two companies so that constraints on the freedom of the individual are illustrated.

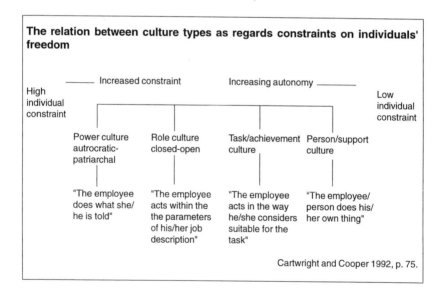

Cartwright and Cooper 1992, p. 75.

With their culture typology Cartwright and Cooper have developed a tool for culture audits which they offer to negotiators and decision-makers to use prior to acquisitions and mergers. However, it can be questioned whether specific companies so unequivocally can be identified as belonging to one of the four culture types. It also can be questioned whether the suggested cultural analyses are feasible before the purchase. Finally, it can be questioned whether Cartwright and Cooper's culture typologies and other categories are good tools with a high prognostic value. Some at least of our case studies indicate that their models would not have been the right tool to predict the course the integration process in fact took.

In one of our case companies, NKT-Electronics, the Danish top management had a great influence on the choice of potential purchasers. Here the managers really thought over which organizational culture would best match the Danish company's. They were convinced though that precisely the foreign company that decided to purchase them, the US-company DSC Communications, would be a good partner, also at a cultural level. The Danish managing directors had the opinion that DSC's organizational culture in many ways was more similar to their own than that of the Danish Holding company of which they had been a part: *"When it comes to the point, indeed we know very little about DSC's organizational culture until now. But we imagine that we fit very well. It was easy to communicate with the financial managers and lawyers in DSC during the negotiations. They were outspoken, frank and direct, and that is what we are, too"*. And *"We are two teenage companies with cultures which have a great many similarities as regards our relations to employees, to customers and to the global market"*. The Danish managing directors expected the foreign company, which also produced high-tech electronic products, to be more empathetic and concerned with their situation and their way of working, and that the purchase would give the Danish company a greater autonomy in economic aspects and better possibilities.

In Cartwright and Cooper's terminology, the Danish company perceived its own organizational culture as a *task culture,* and the Danish managers' first impressions of DSC Communications were that its organizational culture could also be described as a *task culture.* The former owners of NKT-Electronics, a large old Danish concern, NKT-Holding, were described by the managing directors in NKT- Electronics as bureaucratic and inflexible in relation to the demands that global competition makes on product development and marketing of high-tech products. In Cartwright and Cooper's terminology, NKT Holding was described as a *role culture.*

But the Danish managers' expectation that the integration process between NKT-Electronics and DSC Communications would be without friction, were not fulfilled. The two Danish managing directors left the company during the first year because of co-operation problems with the American owners, and the integration process is still characterized by great difficulties and many frictions. There could be various explanations: It is possible that the Danish managers based their assumptions of a cultural fit on a cultural analysis that was far too superficial. And very soon after the acquisition great economic problems appeared because of seriously delayed development of some products. The foreign company was very dissatisfied with the economic results in the Danish company and maybe therefore decided to involve more foreign employees in the Danish company than they had originally planned to do (e.g. in daily management and financial control). It is likely that in any case these interventions would have created a conflict and a clash of interests between the Danish and the American companies, even if there were some similarities with respect to organizational cultures.

Yet another example showing that Cartwright and Cooper's models are not always applicable comes from another of our case companies, a mobile telephone company, Dancall, which the British electronics concern Amstrad acquired in 1993. It is our impression that the integration process passed off without severe conflicts and problems. But according to Cartwright and Cooper the two should have expected a very difficult process. Of course, it is difficult for us as outsiders to describe and characterize the organizational cultures in Amstrad and Dancall before the purchase, solely because we did not get access to Dancall before December 1994, a year after Amstrad's acquisition. But our empirical data give us grounds to state that Amstrad very much resembles what Cooper and Cartwright call a *power culture,* with its charismatic and autocratic owner and CEO, Alan Sugar, whereas Dancall, before the acquisition, might be characterized as an example of a *task culture,* according to Cartwright and Cooper's terminology.

The interviewees at Dancall, both Danish employees and British managers, told us that the autonomy of Dancall has decreased in several areas after the acquisition. Right from the start Amstrad introduced tight financial control, and the British managing director at Dancall did not continue the previous consensus-oriented managerial style. As already mentioned, Cartwright and Cooper assume that an acquisition which results in more constraints on the individual will typically meet serious problems and strong resistance from the employees. But it did not happen at Dancall. This means that a cultural analysis according to Cartwright and Cooper's model would have given an incorrect prediction of the integration process. How can we explain what happened at Dancall?

If we take a look at the specific circumstances, Dancall was in a very special situation before Amstrad's purchase. The foreign acquiring company had a strong power position because Dancall had suspended its payments a month before. It meant that the Danish employees were employed in a new company, seen from a legal point of view. And even though the majority had also been employed at Dancall before its suspension of payments, they did not expect that the conditions of appointment would be the same in every detail.

On the contrary, several groups of employees showed a willingness to accept altered conditions, in particular the unskilled workers in the production division accepted to give up bonus agreements. These workers, who had for a while been confronted by a future of long-term unemployment, perceived the acquiring company and its representatives in Denmark as Dancall's "saviours", who had made the future existence of the company possible and so ensured continued employment for the employees.

This interpretation gained even more strength as the workers realized that Amstrad intended to continue production in Denmark, manifested by the purchase of new machines for production and plans for an expansion of the production area. Against this background, a majority of the workers interpreted the organizational changes, for example the initially very tight financial control, as something positive, even though it resulted in a decrease of autonomy. Thus, the workers interpreted such initiatives as signs that the new managing director, an Englishman who had been put into this job by the foreign concern, was a strong, decisive and visible leader. In contrast, the previous Danish management was regarded as the "villains" in the events – because they had "allowed the safe to stand open" and thus drained the company of the necessary capital for continued research and development. In addition, according to the workers, there had been too many "chiefs" previously.

The situation of the engineers in the research and development division is quite different. It was the group of engineers, who in the summer 1993 took the initiative to contact potential purchasers of Dancall, among them the Amstrad concern. In this initiative they showed their identification with the company and their wish to keep the working partnership. At the same time they were very much aware of their qualifications, and they knew that they could get jobs in other electronics companies, because the majority of the group had received one or more offers during the month when the negotiations took place with Amstrad, among others. They knew that it was their know-how in the new GSM-technology which Amstrad found attractive, who wanted an entry to the growing global market for mobile telephones. Therefore the group of engineers did not accept any reduction of their wages or alterations of their conditions of appointment. They were very critical about any approach from the top management to reduce their autonomy and freedom in work. On the other hand, the management of Dancall, as part of the Amstrad concern, was well aware of the strategic importance of the engineers to the future of the company. Consequently the management preferred to comply with most of the plans and wishes from the engineer group instead of creating new conflicts. The engineers showed their commitment to the company as a workplace in a very critical situation, when they made the decisive choice to contact potential purchasers and thereby showed their identification with the company. But what they seemed to find most important, interesting and challenging were technical issues, the development of new products, and the possibility of continuing their work as a group. The question of whether Dancall, Cetelco or Maxon had appointed them was of secondary importance.

This Dancall case also shows that it can be problematic to assume a homogeneous, relatively stable and coherent organizational culture. In Dancall we observed several subcultures. If we just keep to the two groups mentioned above, the unskilled workers and the engineers, they had very little in common, both from the point of view of their interests in the company and as regards how they perceived the company and interpreted the initiatives of the foreign management. They had very little personal contact with each other, they were working in different buildings, so even at a physical level there were only few points of contact and very little communication. We therefore acquire a much more realistic and multifaceted picture of the company by using a so-called 'differentiation perspective' on the organization.

In „Cultures in Organizations" (1992), Joanne Martin has categorized different approaches to cultural analysis from a general overview of how a culture is perceived and delimited. Here she examines three different perspectives in organizational culture research: the integration perspective, the differentiation perspective and eventually the fragmentation perspective, which will not concern us here.

Within the *integration perspective* the emphasis is on harmony and homogeneity – that is particularly what is looked for when a culture is analysed. A set of themes (often formulated as values and basic assumptions) is described as common for all members in the organizational culture, irrespective of their position in the hierarchy. It is assumed that an organization-wide consensus exists. In the integration perspective, it is assumed that people are aware of what they are doing and why they do it. Organizations are described as rational systems, where clarity and transparency prevail. There is no room in the integration perspective for being concerned with ambiguity. On the contrary, the function of culture as a product of sense-making activity is to avoid anxiety, to control the uncontrollable and make the uncertain predictable. In this way culture helps to control actions and circumstances that could potentially threaten or disrupt the harmony. The integration perspective, which has many similarities with the classic anthropological cultural concept, is typically found in representatives of a value-oriented view of culture; in the field of organizational culture, for example, in Deal and Kennedy (1982), Peters and Waterman (1982), and Schein (1986); within the research field of comparative management, for example in

Hofstede (1992) and within the research field of mergers and acquisitions, for example in Cartwright and Cooper (1992).

The *differentiation perspective* does not deny the existence of a certain degree of similarities, consistencies and unities in the organization. But here efforts are made to investigate the organization from various subcultural perspectives, in order to focus on and investigate differences in power and conflicts of interests between groups of organization members and how these influence groups' interpretations of the organizational reality. In this way, the differentiation perspective will often, for example, help to make visible the perspective on organizations that members without power or status apply to the management. It is thus assumed that subcultures exist – which in turn can be mutually in conflict or in harmony – within the organization. In cases of conflict between subcultures, it is assumed that the members of the individual subcultures are aware of what the disagreements are about. In this way, clarity within the individual subcultures prevails; ambiguity is to be found in the interface between them. The differentiation perspective is thus sceptical about the idea that consensus exists organization-wide, even though there can be consensus within the individual subcultures. It is also assumed that interpretation of themes and practices will often be inconsistent and that there can be disagreement between the expressed values and the actual practice.

I would argue that a differentiation perspective offers a more subtle and many-faceted picture of the Dancall company. It makes a lot of smaller cultural communities visible, subcultures reflecting different professions and divisions, as well as gender and generation differences. Some of these subcultures exist within the company, others cross borders between companies as well as regional and national borders. This is true, for example, when engineers co-operate in a transnational project group, as well as when sales and marketing divisions from several countries work together in a joint effort to market a product.

6. From inter-cultural communication to inter-discourse system communication

In analyses of intercultural communication situations it might be fruitful to narrow the focus to subcultural systems contrasting and conflicting with one another. In some of the above-mentioned examples from our empirical findings I have introduced the concept "subculture" in order to examine the idea that communication between employees within a company could easily be perceived as "corporate communication", and thereby as a manifestation of a "corporate culture". Even if articulations of common values and shared assumptions related to an organizational culture can be observed, they might interfere with explicit values and tacit cultural assumptions belonging to different subcultures: Professional subcultures such as engineers or salesmen; *generations* cf. the difference between the middle-aged managing directors and the young employees with parental duties; or *gender*, cf. the difference between the unskilled female workers and the male foremen in the production division and the female secretaries and the male managing directors.

In the research project *Cultural Contacts and Foreign Acquisitions* we started looking for theoretical concepts within comparative management studies and studies of organizational culture. With business economy as a point of departure it seemed as if Scollon & Scollon, 1995, could offer a more interesting and fruitful approach to the issues we were interested in. They argue that communication takes place across boundaries between groups who cannot only be characterized as subcultures, but as discourse systems, too. From this point of view, intercultural communication might better be analysed as communication between different and competing discourse systems.

But what is a discourse system? According to Scollon & Scollon, the four characteristics which define a discourse system are as follows:

1. "Members will hold a common ideological position and recognize a set of extra-discourse features which define them as a group (*ideology*).

2. Socialization is accomplished primarily through these preferred forms of discourse (*socialization*).

3. A set of preferred forms of discourse serves as banners or symbols of membership and identity (*forms of discourse*).

4. Face relationships are prescribed for discourse among members or between members and outsiders (*face systems*)." (Scollon & Scollon, 1995, p. 98)

What is new about Scollon & Scollon's concept of a discourse system? Just as Hofstede does, they emphasize the interdependence between *ideologies* or worldviews and *socialization* processes. However, it is my impression that they make use of the classic anthropological concept of culture, and that their concept of discourse systems has certain similarities with a concept of subcultures. Discourse systems appear to be relatively stable, homogenous and coherent systems, even though Scollon and Scollon's most elaborated analysis of a discourse system, the Utilitarian discourse system[7], indeed is a clear-cut example of a historical construction. I would also argue that generation and gender discourse systems have been radically transformed during the last decades. So we need to dynamize their concept of discourse systems and emphasize that it is constructed in an ongoing negotiation.

Model of a discourse system

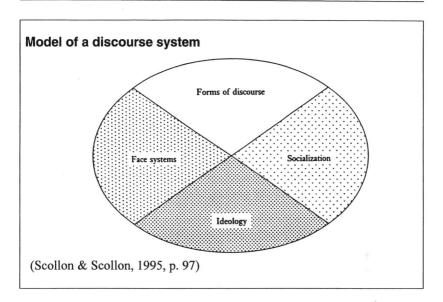

(Scollon & Scollon, 1995, p. 97)

What nevertheless makes Scollon and Scollon´s approach interesting is the fact that they add something new to the other analytical approaches introduced in this article. When they incorporate two further aspects in their concept of a discourse system. With the concept *'forms of discourse'*, one gets the opportunity to focus on the preferred forms of communication which characterize the social practice of a certain group. And in this way you can go further into the study of the use of language than most approaches within the research field of intercultural communication until now have done. For example you could focus on the linguistic realization of face strategies, patterns/ types of cohesion, rhetorical strategies, functions of language as information vs. relation, expressions of and concerns about group harmony and individual welfare, non-verbal communication etc. (Cf. Scollon & Scollon 1995, p. 171).

The concept of face in interconnection with the other three concepts, makes it possible to analyse how groups define themselves in relationship to others, and how the ongoing negotiation of the social relations in the communication processes is also a negotiation on involvement and independence and on ingroup-outgroup relationships.

In the project *Cultural Contacts and Foreign Acquisitions* we have not made any systematic observations of conversation between Danish and foreign employees, nor have we collected any texts which can serve as examples of intercultural communication. Therefore I will not here go further with the concept *forms of discourse*, but I am convinced that it could be fruitful to make new investigations using this concept as an umbrella for communication studies done from a linguistic point of view.

On the other hand, I will briefly discuss the concept of *face*. The theoretical concept was invented by the American sociologist, Erving Goffman (1955), and later taken over by sociolinguists like Brown & Levinson (1978), who used it in order to formulate a theory of politeness strategies. Later, this concept has been used in studies of conflict styles in intercultural communication between Americans and Asians, for example by Ting-Toomey (1988). In the model of facework she distinguishes between *self-face concerns* and *other-face concerns*, and between what she calls the need of a positive face, stressing *association* with a group, and the need of a negative face, stressing *dissociation* from others.

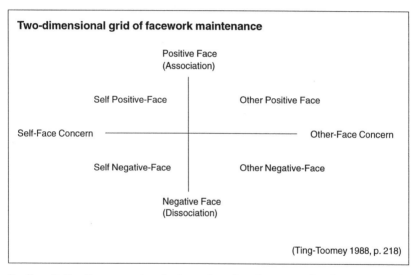

Two-dimensional grid of facework maintenance

Positive Face
(Association)

Self Positive-Face   Other Positive Face

Self-Face Concern   Other-Face Concern

Self Negative-Face   Other Negative-Face

Negative Face
(Dissociation)

(Ting-Toomey 1988, p. 218)

Scollon & Scollon go a step further when they integrate the *face*-concept in their model of a discourse system. They emphasize that the question of whether you are able to handle *face* issues in a specific communication situation has to do with whether you can balance between what they call *involvement* (Ting-Toomey *association*) and *independence* (Ting-Toomey *dissociation*). They are seen as two fundamental needs which all interlocutors are assumed to have in every communication situation and which they try to fulfil. What is interesting, according to Scollon & Scollon, is that in intercultural communication you can observe differences in the ways people choose to meet these needs, due to the culture they are socialized into, and due to the cultural context of the specific communication situation.

It seems to me that the concepts of *involvement* and *independence* as two fundamental needs might also be fruitful if you turn from communication between individuals to communication between an acquiring company and an acquired company.

I will try to use the *face* concept to elucidate some critical events reported in interviews with the employees. Before I make this attempt, I will, once more, make the reservation that the only available empirical data are interview. Danish managers' and employees' retrospective constructions of how they experienced and interpreted communication situations which could be characterized as critical incidents in the integration process.

In Dancall several employees on their own initiative told us about a situation a short time after Amstrad's purchase of the Danish company. The owner and CEO of Amstrad, Alan Sugar, had announced a visit to the new business unit. All the Danish managers were standing outside the entrance to the main building in order to receive him and greet him as he jumped out of the car at the parking lot in front of the entrance to the building. But they were amazed when they realized that he did not intend to greet them. The only person he greeted was the British managing director. For the Danish managers, who might be characterized as relatively egalitarian, this act was interpreted as a deliberate rejection of their friendly attempt to show concern for Alan Sugar, and to signal their feeling of involvement and solidarity with him as representative of Amstrad (cf. the widespread interpretation of Amstrad as Dancall's '*saviour*'). The foreign owner's lack of attention to their friendly gesture was interpreted as a lack of involvement and as a lack of politeness. This situation could have become a source of profound doubt among the Danish employees if the managing director had not expressed a concern for the Danes' face in his management of the company in many other ways both the need of the Danish company to maintain relative autonomy in relation to the Amstrad concern – a need that the expatriate managing director also had himself – and the need for involvement and identification between him and the employees, (cf. the statements made by the workers and the managing director, both expressing a feeling of "*We did it together*").

However, when the acquiring company attempts to demonstrate solidarity in an early phase of the integration process, it can also be interpreted as an offence to the acquired company. At least some of the employees in NKT-Elektronics felt uncomfortable at the dinner party that took place just after DSC Communications' purchase of the Danish company. In order to celebrate the acquisition, the American company had invited all the Danish employees and their spouses, from management to engineers and technicians to secretaries and production workers, to a party with a three-course dinner at a hotel in Copenhagen. The Americans had brought baseball caps printed with the names of the two companies for all the people at the party. The Americans' intention was probably to signal interdependence and team spirit, in Scollon & Scollon's terminology *involvement*. But according to our interviews, some of the Danes found it comical, ridiculous or even humiliating to have to put on a baseball cap when they had dressed up in good clothes for the occasion. They felt uncomfortable wearing the baseball cap, a symbol of their acceptance of the American culture and lifestyle, an act intended to signal identification with the foreign acquiring company, which had not yet had time to develop. At the time when the purchase was announced, at least some of the groups of employees who had not in any way been involved in the negotiations still had a feeling of anxiety about the future: What would happen to their division of the company? Would the production division be closed and the production moved to other countries as it happened in another electronics company acquired by the American Motorola? DSC Communications already had a European centre for sales and marketing. Would there be a Danish division of sales and marketing in the future? With these sorts of reservation towards the foreign company, these employees had a much greater need to express their *independence* and to be met by the foreigners' concern for this face need.

These above-mentioned examples demonstrate how the concept of *face* can elucidate some communicative and interpretative aspects of some critical incidents in the integration process.

7. A Quest for cultural identity – the social constructionist paradigm

Earlier in this article I have presented and discussed different concepts and theoretical models which are often offered as tools to predict how the integration process will proceed, so that the companies can avoid major problems related to differences in the companies' and the employees' national value systems or differences related to different organizational cultures.

Through analyses of some of our empirical findings I have questioned the assumption that the cultural aspects of the integration process can be characterized by contacts, or even clashes, between different national cultures and organizational cultures, perceived as contacts between well-defined, relatively stable, harmonious and coherent value systems. An assumption made on the basis of the classic concept of culture which was introduced in section 1.

Now I will elaborate a quite different perspective on culture, the social constructionist approach, which was also introduced in section 1: Focus is thereby moved from cultural differences which are assumed to be objective. In contrast, attention is now drawn to the way employees in a company *interpret* certain critical incidents in an integration process as an expression of "cultural clashes" and thereby construct a certain reality framing their actions. Culture is perceived as "the constantly ongoing attempt of the collective to define itself and its situation" (Kleppestø, 1993, p. 23). This implies that culture is regarded as an interpretative process rather than a relatively constant value and norm structure.

In this interpretative process the employees in the two companies not only communicate about certain issues like principles of financial control, new report systems or salary systems (*content communication*). At the same time they communicate about how they perceive themselves and the other part, both as individuals, as a division in the company, as a professional group and as a whole company *(relation communication).*[8] This communication about "who are we?" and "how do we look upon the others?" can be seen as a quest for cultural identity. Identity-creating processes are always characterized by a quest for similarities: what brings us together and why do we feel a kind of solidarity within this group? But simultaneously, identities are constructed by definitions that emphasize cultural differences that differentiate one from other groups. From this social constructionist point of view, culture is a community of shared meanings that are constructed in the process of a group or an organization trying to define themselves and their actual situation.

On this theoretical basis, the Norwegian-Swedish researcher Stein Kleppestø has conducted a comprehensive case study of two merging Swedish companies, Bofors and FFV Ordnance, where he focused on the integration process and the communication between the companies (Kleppestø 1993). Kleppestø investigated how the integration process affects the employees' ideas about their cultural identity. He showed that the acquisition in itself implies that employees' need for a cultural affiliation and an identity increases, as their job situation and their affiliation to the acquired company seems to be threatened. He also demonstrated that in the role of consultant it could be essential to look at the constructed patterns of interpretation and at aspects of the relation communication between the two companies, in order to improve the cultural and communicative aspects of the integration process.

Several empirical findings from our case studies corroborate these ideas. The economic and strategic starting situation of the Danish company is crucial for the employees' interpretation of the relationship to the new parent company. Has the company been bought as an attractive partner with a particular potential for continued development and/or production? Or does the value of the company consist exclusively in representing a short-term possibility of profit for the parent company, for example through transfer of technological competence from the subsidiary company, which would then in the long term risk losing its own reason for existence?

In our interviews we noticed that the foreign company and its representatives in some cases were spoken about in a way that indicated that the foreign acquisition actualized some well-known national stereotypes: "*Ordnung muss sein*" was mentioned several times in connection with a German acquisition, to illustrate the primary area for the experienced differences and difficulties. The Germans were interpreted as being bureaucratic, as people who put great emphasis on formalising all work procedures, and who replaced the flat decision-making structure and delegation of responsibility typical of the Danish entrepreneurial culture with a pronounced hierarchical structure and top-down communication. The experienced German managerial style was retrospectively summarized by an interviewee in the expression that "*you could hear the tramp of jackboots in the corridors*".

In another of our case companies, NKT-Electronics, where the American acquiring company according to the Danish interviewees dominated the Danish management and did not show any kind of understanding of the Danish way of life, we heard statements like "*The Americans think that all that is big is also good. Therefore they want to change our production systems into mass production and work on a production line, where the Danish workers for years have been accustomed to autonomous working teams, and are very fond of them. In order to put their omnipotent plans for our company in some kind of perspective, I decided to quote one of Piet Hein's Grooks[9] at a meeting with some of the American managing directors. But I do not think they got my point.*" In order to throw these negative expressions in relief, it should be mentioned that the acquired companies do not always meet the foreign acquiring company with fear and other negative attitudes and with a conscious effort to maintain what they experience as a certain Danish organizational culture and managerial style. On the contrary, companies like NKT-Electronics were looking forward to the future co-operation with DSC Communications with great optimism. Interviewees stated that they did not expect major difficulties due to national differences, in an outspoken remark: "*Americans are white people just as we are, and we all speak English, so why should we meet any problems?*"

Ideas about the cultural identity of your own organization often function in just the same way as the national stereotypes. The Danish managers in NKT-Electronics described their own managerial style in this way: "*we talk about an awful lot of things, we are willing to go and have an open and honest discussion about them and listen to one other, without focus on the interlocutor's position in the company hierarchy. What we are concerned about is the need to create consensus about the decisions, and an understanding among the employees of why these decisions have been made. But what the American company puts into practice is management by fear"*. In accordance with this interpretation the American chairman of the board was experienced as a self-willed and autocratic leader and by some of the Danish managers was given the nickname *Roi Soleil/ Sun King.*

The dominating trend within the research field of mergers and acquisitions has focussed on cultural resistance and psychological barriers to integration and organizational change. The social constructionist approach on the other hand elucidates that the ongoing interpretation processes taking place in the integration of the merging companies gradually change and reorganize the perception of self and the other so that it better matches the new reality.

In the process of seeking to define cultural identity, the positions and interpretations are not fixed. The subjectively experienced boundaries between cultures and groups are fluent and in constant movement. If a conflict situation between two companies comes to an end - for example because of a joint economic success – it suddenly becomes less important to emphasize the cultural identity as a Dane, as an exponent of a particular Danish management style and of the particular organizational culture of company X.

Generally, our impression from the interviews is that the relationship with the foreign acquiring company and the way their „otherness" are interpreted change in the course of time. Stereotypical ideas about other nations or other organizational cultures are most prevalent at the beginning, before the employees have had personal contact with the foreigners, or in their very first meetings with them. Here the stereotypical ideas about nations act as a filter for the perception of foreigners, and they are used as simple explanations of behaviour that strikes the Danes as strange or irritating. Later the stereotypical ideas about particular national characters recede and other interpretative patterns emerge which give access to more multifaceted images of and experiences of persons and groups in specific contexts. Then the experienced differences in attitudes and behaviour are interpreted and explained to a greater extent in other ways, for example as an expression of the economic interests, strategic aims, or as an expression of certain employees' personality. So it is no longer Germans in general that are bureaucratic or dictatorial. But the management of the parent company may for example represent a traditional authoritarian management style or they are, for some reason, unpleasant, inflexible, bad at listening and having a dialogue with the Danes, or whatever the problem is.

When the integration process goes well, new interpretative patterns emerge after a while. For example expressions of a we-feeling, including groups of Danish and foreign employees in company X will emerge, while the more stereotypical ideas will now only be used in order to interpret the competing company Y's attitudes and behaviour. When the group of unskilled workers at Dancall with pride expressed a statement like *"We succeeded in transforming Dancall into a healthy and prosperous company"*, they identify with the efforts of the British managing director who in another interview stated: *"The Danish workers are simply more clever than the British. Therefore we managed to set Dancall on its feet again"*. Here an alliance between the managing director and the workers has been established.

Concluding remarks

I have discussed certain tools for cultural analysis, which are based on ideas about national cultures and organizational cultures as uniform, coherent, value systems. I have questioned these ideas, referring both to the sub-cultures linked to departments, professions and other communities of interest and meaning and found within a nation, and to the trans-national sub-cultures, to which business people within internationally working companies can belong.

The analysis of empirical findings related to perceived differences in national cultures and organizational cultures has elucidated the difficulties related to the concepts of culture. They have also demonstrated that the situations in the companies are so complex that they cannot be handled with such broad concepts as "national culture" and "organizational culture".

I am convinced that national and organizational differences often play an important role in the integration process in companies. But I have argued that culture must not be understood as something objective and given, which a nation or an organization has. Moreover, I have questioned the assumption implicit in many studies of intercultural communication and comparative management that national differences always make a difference. Furthermore I have shown that it can be very difficult to state that organizational changes in the acquired companies should necessarily be interpreted as a result of contacts with another national culture. Some of the observed organizational changes might have been carried out in a Danish setting, too, simply as a consequence of the company's internal development.

As an alternative, I would recommend that attention be directed to the integration process, and that it is regarded as a process where the companies communicate to each other and with each other about what they perceive as their cultural identity. It is a communication process that at first can help to create and maintain assumptions about themselves and the others in professional groups, departments and the whole organization, and in the long run, to develop new visions of a community of joint interests and tasks.

The general statement to be made on the basis of the above mentioned examples and statements from the case studies is that the integration process must also be viewed as a communication process. As a process where groups in the companies construct various self-images, where they make changing interpretations of the organizational reality and of the relation between the two companies. Thus I have presented a *relational* and a *process-oriented* approach to cultural analysis.

Notes

[1]   This article is based on an interdisciplinary reasearch project Cultural Contacts and Foreign Acquisitions. A special thank to my collegue, associate professor Martine Cardel Gertsen for inspiring discussions in relation to our collaboratory efforts in writing the articles, Gertsen & Søderberg 1996a, Gertsen & Søderberg 1996b. Another version of this article has been published in Gertsen & Søderberg 1998a.

[2]   For a more detailed introduction to the distinction between culture as empirical category and analytical implication, see e.g. Hastrup, 1989 and Hastrup, 1995.

[3]   Martine Cardel Gertsen has a research background in intercultural management, Jens Erik Torp in international economics, and the author of this article in intercultural communication.

[4]   Kleppestø, 1992, is a comprehensive study of the international literature on cultural aspects of the integration process. Gertsen, Søderberg & Torp, 1998, is an updated critical examination of this research approach.

[5]   Cf the widespread thinking in dualisms between sense and sensitivity, body and soul, spiritual and secular etc.

[6]   In Gertsen & Søderberg 1998b crital incidents in the integration process has been analyzed using national business systems as a theoretical frame of reference. Cartwright & Cooper, 1992

[7]   Op cit p 98-117.

[8]   Watzlawick, Beavin & Jackson, 1967.

[9]   *Denmark seen from foreign land, looks but like a grain of sand - Denmark as we Danes perceive it, is so big you won't believe it.* (Piet Hein)

Bibliography

Altendorf, D.M. (1986): *When Cultures Clash: A Case Study of the Texaco Take-Over of Getty Oil and the Impact of Acculturation on the Acquired Firm.* Ph.D. Dissertation, University of Southern California, Los Angeles.

Argyris, C. and Schön, D. (1978): *Organizational Learning.* London: Addison Westley.

Barth, F. (1969): Introduction. In: Barth, F. (ed.): *Ethnic groups and boundaries*. Oslo: Universitetsforlaget.

Barth, F (1994a): Analysen af kultur i komplekse samfund. In Barth, F.: *Manifestasjon og prosess*. Oslo: Universitetsforlaget.

Barth, F. (1994b): Er verdier virkelige? Naturalisme som utfordring i antropologisk verditilskrivelse, In Barth, F.: *Manifestasjon og prosess,*. Oslo: Universitetsforlaget.

Brown, P. & Levinson, S. (1978): Universals in language usage. Politiness phenomena. In E. Goody (Ed.): *Questions and politeness: Strategies in social interaction*. Cambridge: Cambridge University Press.

Cartwright, S. and Cooper, C.L. (1992): *Mergers and acquisitions: the human factor*. Oxford: Butterworth-Heinemann Ltd.

Cartwright, S. and Cooper, C.L. (1993): The role of culture compatability in successful organizational marriage. In: *Academy of Management Executive*, 7 (2), 57-70.

Czarniawska-Joerges, B. (1992): *Exploring Complex Organizations. A Cultural Perspective*. Newbury, London: Sage.

Davis, R.B. (1968): Compatability in corporate marriages. In: *Harvard Business Review*, 46 (4), 86-93.

Deal, T.E. & Kennedy, A. (1982): *Corporate Cultures*. Reading: Addison Wesley.

Downing, S. and Hunt, J.W. (1990): Mergers, Acquisitions and Human Resource Management. In: *The International Journal of Human Resource Management*, vol. 1, no. 1, September, 195-209.

Eriksen, T.H. (1993): *Ethnicity and Nationalism. Anthropological Perspectives*. London: Pluto Press.

Gertsen, M.C. (1990): *Fjernt fra Danmark. Interkulturel kompetence i teori og praksis*. København: Handelshøjskolens forlag.

Gertsen, M.C. (1995): Intercultural Training as In-Service Training. A Discussion of Possible Approaches. In: Aarup Jensen, A., Jæger, K. and Lorentsen A. (Eds.): *Intercultural Competence. A New Challenge for Language Teachers and Trainers in Europe*, Vol. II. Aalborg: Aalborg University Press.

Gertsen, M.C. & Søderberg, A.-M. (1996a): *Changes in Companies' Organization and Identity - Theoretical Considerations in Connection with a Series of Case Studies of Foreign Acquisitions of Danish Companies*. Working Paper no.8, Department of Intercultural Communication and Management, Copenhagen Business School.

Gertsen, M.C. & Søderberg, A.-M. (1996b): Interkulturelle læreprocesser ved internationale virksomhedsopkøb. In: Gullestrup, H. & Lorentsen, A. (Eds.): *Interkulturel kompetence*. Aalborg: Aalborg Universitetsforlag.

Gertsen, M.C. & Søderberg, A.-M. (1998): Kulturelle aspekter ved fusioner og virksomhedsopkøb. In: Strandgaard Pedersen, J. (Ed.): *Fusioner*. København: Jurist- og Økonomforbundets forlag.

Gertsen, M.C., Søderberg, A.-M. & Torp, J.E. (1995): *Kulturmøder i forbindelse med virksomheders internationaliseringsproces. Projektbeskrivelse.* Working Paper no. 1, Department of Intercultural Communication and Management, Copenhagen Business School.

Gertsen, M.C., Søderberg, A.M. & Torp, J.E. (1995): *Cultural Contacts in Foreign Acquisitions.* Occasional Paper. Research Workshop: The Cultural Dimensions of International Mergers and Acquisitions. 27-28 August 1996, Department of Intercultural Communication and Management, Copenhagen Business School.

Gertsen, M.C., Søderberg, A.-M. & Torp, J.E. (Eds.) (1998):*Cultural Dimensions of International Acquisitions*. Berlin & New York:Walther de Gruyter.

Gertsen, M.C., Søderberg, A.-M. & Torp, J.E. (1998): Different Approaches to the Understanding of Culture in Mergers and Acquisitions. In: Gertsen, M., Søderberg, A.-M. & Torp, J.E. (Eds.): *Cultural Dimensions of International Acquisitions*. Berlin & New York: Walther de Gruyter.

Gertsen, M.C. & Søderberg, A.-M (1998): *Integration Processes Following International Acquisitions in Denmark: A Case Study of European Organizational Integration.* Working Paper no 64, Department of Intercultural Communication and Management, Copenhagen Business School.

Gioia, D.A. (1986): Symbols, Scripts and Sensemaking: Creating Meaning in the Organizational Experience. In: Sims, Gioia et al.: *The Thinking Organisation: Dynamics of Organisational Social Cognition.* San Francisco: Jossey-Bass.

Goffman, E. (1955): On face-work: An analysis of ritual elements in social interaction. In: *Psychiatry: Journal for Study of International Processes.*

Hampden-Turner, C. & Trompenaars, F. (1993): *The Seven Cultures of Capitalism. Value Systems for Creating Wealth in the united States, Japan, Germany, France, Great Britain, Sweden and the Netherlands*. New York: Currency Doubleday.

Hannerz, U. (1992): *Cultural Complexity*. New York: Columbia University Press.

Hannerz, U. (1990): Cosmopolitans and Locals in World Culture. In: Featherstone, M. (Ed.): *Global Culture. Nationalism, Globalization and Modernity*. London: Sage.

Hastrup, K. (1992): *Det antropologiske projekt - om forbløffelse.* København: Gyldendal.

Hastrup ,K. (1989): Kultur som analytisk kategori. In: Hastrup & Ramløv (Eds.): *Kulturanalyse. Fortolkningens forløb i antropologien*. København: Akademisk forlag.

Hastrup, K (1995): *A passage to anthropology between experience and theory*. London and New York: Routledge.

Hofstede, G. (1984): *Culture's Consequences. International Differences in Work-Related Values*. Beverly Hills: Sage.

Hofstede, G. (1992): *Kulturer og organisationer - overlevelse i en grænseoverskridende verden*. København: Schultz Erhvervsbøger.

Inkeles, A. & Levinson, D.J. (1954): National character: the study of modal personality and sociocultural systems. In: Lindsey, G. & Aronson, E. (eds.): *The Handbook of Social Psychology*. Reading: Addison Esley.

Kleppestø, S. (1992): *Kulturell integration vid uppköp och fusion: En litteraturstudie*. Lund: Institutet för Ekonomisk Forskning. Working Paper Series 10.

Kleppestø, S. (1993): *Kultur och identitet vid företagsuppköp och fusioner*. Stockholm: Nerenius och Santérus.

Kluckhohn, C. (1962): Universal Categories of Culture. In: S. Tax (ed.): *Anthropology Today*. Chicago: University of Chicago Press.

Kluckhohn, C. & Strodtbeck, F. (1961): *Variations in value orientations*. Evanston: Row, Peterson and Co.

Konkurrencerådet (1995): *Fusioner og virksomhedsovertagelser 1994*. København: Konkurrencerådet.

Kroeber, A. & Kluckhohn, C. (1952): *Culture: a critical review of concepts and definitions*. Cambridge: Harvard University.

Kunda, G. (1992): *Engineering Culture*. Philadelphia: Temple University Press.

Liep, J. & Fog Olwig, K (1994): Kulturel kompleksitet. In Liep & Fog Olwig (Ed.): *Komplekse liv. Kulturel mangfoldighed i Danmark*. København: Akademisk Forlag.

Martin, J. (1992): *Cultures in Organizations. Three Perspectives*. New York: Oxford University Press.

Parsons, T. & Shils, E.A. (1951): *Towards a general theory of action*. Cambridge: Harvard University Press.

Peters, T. & Waterman, R.H. (1982): *In Search of Excellence*. New York: Harper & Row.

Ronen, S. (1986): *Comparative and Multinational Management*. New York: John Wiley & Sons.

Sales, A.L. and Mirvis, P.H. (1984): When Cultures Collide: Issues in Acquisitions. In: Kimberley, J. and Quinn, R. (Eds.): *New Futures: The challenge of managing corporate transitions*. Homewood, Illinois: Dow Jones and Irwin.

Schein, E. (1986): *Organisationskultur og ledelse.* København: Valmuen.

Schultz, M. (1995): *On studying organizational cultures.* Berlin & New York: Walther de Gruyter.

Scollon, R. & Scollon, S.W.(1995): *Intercultural Communication. A Discourse Approach.* Oxford & Cambridge: Blackwell.

Smircich, L. (1985): Is the concept of culture a paradigm for understanding organizations and ourselves? In: Frost et al. (eds.): *Organizational culture.* California: Sage Publishing.

Søderberg, A.-M. (1993): Turisten og den professionelle rejsende – om antropologisk feltarbejde og kulturanalyse. In: Hjort, Løngreen & Søderberg (Eds.): *Interkulturel kommunikation - spændingsfeltet mellem det globale og det lokale.* København: Samfundslitteratur.

Søderberg, A.-M. og Villemoes, A. (1994): *Undervejs. Sprog, kultur og kommunikation i den erhvervssproglige medarbejders perspektiv.* København: Samfundslitteratur.

Tajfel, H. (1982): *Social identity and intergroup relations.* Cambridge: Cambridge University Press.

Terpstra, V. (1978): *The Cultural Environment of International Business.* Cincinnati: South-Western Publishing Company.

Thyssen, O. (1994): *Kommunikation, kultur og etik.* København: Handelshøjskolens forlag.

Ting-Toomey, S. (1988): Intercultural Conflict Styles. A Face-Negotiation Theory. In: Kim,Y.Y. & Gudykunst, W.B. (Eds.) *Theories in Intercultural Communication.* Newbury Park: Sage.

Trompenaars, F. (1993): *Riding the Waves of Culture. Understanding Culture and Diversity in Business.* London: Nicholas Brealey Publishing.

van Maanen, J. (1988): *Tales of the Field. On Writing Ethnography.* Chicago & London: The University of Chicago Press.

Vestergaard, T.A. (1988): Kultur i dansk kulturforskning. In: Hauge, H. og H. Horstbøll: *Kulturbegrebets kulturhistorie.* Århus: Aarhus Universitetsforlag.

Watzlawick, P., Beavin, J.B. & Jackson, D.D. (1967): *Pragmatics of Human Communication.* New York & London: W.W. Northon & Co.